Praise for
ANXIOUS for AN

"*Anxious for Answers* reads like a temporary escape from your own anxious mind. Dr. Ilene invites you to create a new relationship with anxiety, one that allows you to create a healthy relationship with it. Anxious for Answers is easy to read and provides hands on ways to beat anxiety once and for all. Dr. Ilene gets you rethinking about anxiety!"

~ DR. EDRICA D. RICHARDSON, LMFT

"*Anxious for Answers* serves up a powerful paradigm shift full of transformative potential. Offering practical and relatable wisdom drawn from Bowen Family Systems Theory and her own personal experience, Dr. Ilene guides readers into a new relationship with anxiety and, most meaningfully, with themselves."

~DR. DENISE FOURNIER, LMHC

"In today's overly anxious society and culture, books like *Anxious for Answers* provide us with the tools necessary to cope with all the emotions tied to our personal fears. Dr. Ilene does a brilliant job breaking down the origins of anxiety, how anxiety is perpetuated in our everyday lives, and how to combat it effectively."

~CORINNE DEBACHER, M.Ed

"Dr. Ilene's latest book, *Anxious for Answers*, is a timely addition to furthering our understanding of anxiety. It is a straight forward, easy to understand, and useful guide to managing the stresses of life and relationships, with practical advice and strategies for calming one's heart and quieting one's mind. I highly recommend this book for anyone, clinician and lay person, who wants to learn to be more mature in their ability to manage life's uncertainties, worries and fears. I use it with my graduate students and suggest it to my clients as well. The ability to soothe oneself, quiet the heart and calm the mind are invaluable tools to enhance a person's emotional functioning. At a time when there is so much anxiety, uncertainty and fear, this book arrives as an early Christmas gift. It is a straight forward, easy to understand guide, (supported by clinical theory and case examples) to many of the life stressors and relationship concerns we all have to face. Chock-full of practical advice and strategies to aide people in "holding onto their better self", this is a book that I highly recommend."

~ JIM RUDES, Ph.D., LMFT, LCSW
Associate Professor Barry University

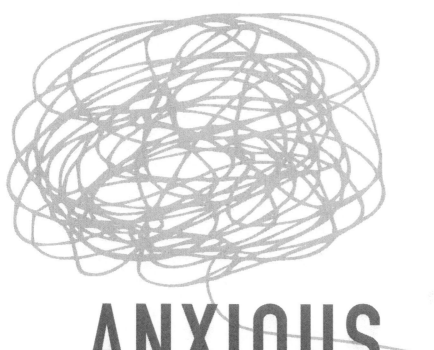

ANXIOUS

FOR ANSWERS

The surprising truth about anxiety,

and how you can

MASTER IT FOR GOOD!

ILENE S. COHEN, PhD

HARTE & CO PUBLISHING • MIAMI FLORIDA

Anxious for Answers: The surprising truth about anxiety, and how you can master it for good!

by Ilene S. Cohen, Ph.D.

Published by Harte & Co Publishing

Editor: Denise Fournier
Book design: BookSavvyStudio.com

Library of Congress Control Number: 2020906523
ISBN: 978-0-9993115-2-3
First Edition
Printed in the United States of America

DEDICATION

To those who suffer from chronic anxiety, remember that you aren't weak or any less of a person because of this. By facing what scares you every single day, you show resilience and strength. This book was written for you.

"The process by which an individual can reduce their level of chronic anxiety depends primarily on learning. The learning depends on having the COURAGE to engage emotionally intense situations repeatedly and to tolerate the anxiety and internal emotional reactivity associated with that engagement. This anxiety associated with **trying to become more of a self, an anxiety of progression** rather than regression."

~ MICHAEL KERR, *Family Evaluation*

CONTENTS

INTRODUCTION

I N MY SOPHOMORE YEAR OF COLLEGE, I was driving home during winter break, when my heart suddenly started beating at a faster pace. It was like I'd just finished a long sprint. I started feeling lightheaded, and white flakes fluttered before my eyes. Frantically, I thought, Am I having a heart attack? *What can I do to stop this? Am I dying?* I tried to take deep breaths, but it was like someone was standing on my rib cage. I struggled to breathe. I pulled my car over to the side of the road, fearing that I'd pass out and hit someone. "Breathe," I told myself. "Just breathe." After what seemed like the longest hour of my life—which, in reality, lasted no more than 5 minutes—my breathing went back to normal. I could see clearly again, and all the fear left my body. "What the hell was that?" I thought to myself. Then I started my car again and kept driving toward home, hoping that had all just been some sort of fluke.

But what happened in the car that day wasn't just a one-time thing— it was just the beginning. I didn't have the knowledge at the time to know that I'd just gone through my first panic attack. It was probably the scariest thing I'd ever experienced. And, of course, I had to be driving alone at the time, on a long road with few exits and no cell service. Naturally, I wondered who would be the first to discover my body. But I didn't die that day. Instead, I started off on a voyage that I never would have volunteered for. And after that, my anxiety didn't stop at panic attacks. It manifested into severe muscle pain, ulcers, extreme people-pleasing, and perfectionism. I silently suffered for years, until one day I decided to seek help and make some changes. I could no longer enjoy my life. I lived in fear of when my next panic attack would strike, and I avoided anything that might make me anxious.

However, once I got help and began to see my progress, I was grateful for everything I had to go through in order to become who I am today. My anxiety took me on an unanticipated joy ride that I never would have imagined for myself. And I'll be honest, I kicked and screamed most of the way. But eventually, I found a sense of motivation and purpose for the work I had to do to get better. Now, it's important for me to mention that this book isn't about me and my story. Though I do provide some examples from my life and the lives of some of my clients, this is ultimately about you, and what you can do to live a less anxious life. My hope is that with the information I provide here, you can find your own way to live with more freedom and flexibility—to live more from yourself.

Lately, everywhere I turn, I hear about people who are struggling with anxiety. When I tell people about the topic of this book, they look at me with a sparkle in their eyes and say something like, "Oh, I struggle with anxiety," or, "My sister suffers from anxiety." It's recently become one of the most commonly diagnosed mental health issues, and it's often treated with psychotropic drugs strong enough to put a horse to sleep. I've often wondered, *Why is anxiety so prevalent now? Why, when we've come so far scientifically and technologically, is it running rampant in our culture?* Compared to people in any other time in history, we live pretty comfortably. We have so many advantages and luxuries, live longer than ever, and have more opportunities than our ancestors could have dreamed of; yet, somehow, we seem to be more anxious than ever before.

Anxiety is pervasive in our culture, but our mainstream way of thinking offers no clear-cut reasons for why this is. Why are our hearts beating outside of our chests in panic when we aren't being chased by a predator? Why are we gasping for air with tightening chests, as we sit in the comfort of our home, watching a Hallmark movie? Why do we feel like we're dying when we aren't? Why are we anxious about a future that hasn't happened yet? About scenarios that will likely never happen? What's going on in our lives and culture that would have us prefer feeling numb over feeling alive?

There's so much accessible information out there, yet we're more lost than ever when it comes to our own suffering. Most of us don't seek change until we're pretty uncomfortable. We ignore it until our problems become almost impossible to handle. So, what's going on in our lives that's creating such suffering? What's getting us so anxious that we can't see all the opportunities and pleasures life has for us? Anxiety can convince even the smartest and most fortunate among us that our lives aren't worth living and that it's too dangerous to get on that flight or walk out that door for a cup of coffee. We might ask ourselves, *What is happening, and how did we come to be so nervous about these seemingly small things?*

I mean, sure, we can find many reasons for our day-to-day stresses, like traffic, sucky jobs, overdrawn bank accounts, natural disasters, terrorism, terrible spouses, mass shootings. It's easy to point our finger at any one of those as the real and only cause of our anxiety. But is the answer that simple? Does it work to say that this is the cause of your anxiety, and now here's a nicely packaged pill or meditation practice that will take away all your uncomfortable anxious feelings? Can it really work that way? Will the panic you get when randomly driving your car, stepping onto a plane, watching a movie, or waking up in the middle of the night in terror all disappear with some medication or breathing practices? It might seem to work at first, and it can certainly be helpful with acute anxiety, but over time, this is just a Band-Aid solution that doesn't solve the real problem of chronic anxiety.

Anxiety is real, and it's present in all living things. But for some people, it's more manageable than for others. While one person might feel a few butterflies in their stomach before a big test, another needs to run to the bathroom every five minutes to throw up. Why do some people have the ability to control or manage their anxiety better than others? Is there something inherently wrong with the people who can't stay calm and keep it together when they're anxious?

In this book, I've taken a close look at these questions. My mission is to show you a new way to think about anxiety that doesn't have you feeling guilty for being the only one on the plane staring down the emergency exit while lamenting that this is your last day on earth. I take a systemic look at anxiety and, with the help of research, show why it happens, how you can deal with it more effectively, and why it's so important to start making real changes now.

After reading this book, you'll become besties with your anxiety. Well…maybe not besties. But you'll definitely have a better understanding of its purpose and presence, without thinking you need to numb yourself for life to feel normal. After reading this book, you'll be more accepting and understanding of why you feel the way you feel, which will help you start conquering your emotions.

Why I'm Writing This Book

The topic of this book is very personal to me. As I said, I've suffered quietly with anxiety for many years of my life. My husband and many of my family members suffer from it as well. But I've found a way to live so that anxiety doesn't dictate my actions anymore. I took the reins of my life back several years ago, and I want the same for anyone who struggles with anxiety. I've seen people suffer for far too long. It's time you take your life back. The life that you deserve to live. The life that so many people before you fought for you to have. The freedom. The laughter. The smiles.

The things we all deeply deserve but can't fully appreciate when we're anxious.

This book is a compilation of research, practical advice, and explanations from the theory I work with in therapy—which has personally saved my life—called the Bowen Family Systems Theory. I cover many topics in this book, and I wrote it for every kind of reader. If you aren't an avid reader, feel free to skip the sections that don't feel relevant for you. However, I strongly recommend that you don't skip the sections on theory, because they will help you understand yourself and appreciate the complexities of anxiety. If you're a hands-on learner, make sure you pay special attention to the activities at the end of each chapter. If you're a fan of research, read those sections first. If you like to read about anything and everything, as I do, take the cover-to-cover approach. I designed this book to offer you everything you need to know about anxiety, but it's up to you to decide which parts apply to you. I've tried to include everything a person can possibly go through when dealing with anxiety, in the hopes that the information can make a difference in your life, as it's done for me and many of my clients. This book offers you a way of learning how to manage your anxiety and finally get your life back. I've seen people make unbelievable transformations through the information I'm sharing here, and I believe that you can do the same. I've learned that how we think about anxiety, and what we do to manage it, make it either a blessing or a curse in our lives. Confronting our anxiety takes courage and determination. If you're brave enough, let's get to it!

CHAPTER 1

ANXIOUS WITHOUT A THREAT

Anxiety is an expression of our survival instinct.

History of Anxiety

I F YOU'RE READING THIS BOOK, I know you have anxiety. But how? Is it because you picked up this particular book? Actually, no. It's because to be alive is to be anxious; there is *no other way.* We all have anxiety—and for a very good reason. In fact, if we weren't anxious by nature, we wouldn't be here right now. In every living thing, anxiety is part of the *survival instinct,* the built-in response to perceived threats. This is what makes us drive carefully in a rainstorm and avoid walking too close to the edge of a cliff. It's our inner alarm system. It helps keep us alive. All living things have it. Even animals, running for their lives from the predators chasing them down, display anxiety. That's what gets them moving. **When seen in this way, anxiety isn't pathological or dysfunctional; it's a natural and appropriate response to a perceived threat.**

You might be wondering, *Why do we still have this instinct?* What purpose does it serve in 2020, when the fear of being some predator's dinner is no longer part of our everyday lives? Haven't we evolved enough to know not to drive too fast in bad weather or hang out in burning buildings? Apparently not. We may have evolved, but our survival instinct is still very much the same as it's always been; if anything, it's become even *more* alert, detecting things other than just immediate threats to our survival. Does knowing this fact make it easier to deal with anxiety? Does it make the anxiety any more tolerable? As a matter of fact, yes, it does. Having a clearer and more logical understanding, all the while knowing why something is happening in your life, provides a path to freedom. The more you understand something and see it for what it is, the less control it will have over you and your life.

A common belief about anxiety is that it's an emotional disorder existing inside of a person, consisting of that person's overthinking, excessive worrying, and fearfulness about the future. Anxiety is listed as a mental disorder, characterized by significant feelings of anxiety and fear. Most of the time, the professionals diagnosing this disorder and the patients suffering from it, don't even think or talk about the origins of anxiety. They don't dig deeper into what's going on; their sole focus is on getting rid of it. And thinking of anxiety as a mental health concern, as something that's inherently wrong with you, isn't particularly helpful when it comes to properly learning how to manage and live with it. The more we judge ourselves or feel bad about our experiences, instead of seeing them in context, the more difficult it is for us to deal with issues when they arise.

It's a fact that anxiety has important adaptive functions for us. However, like most things in life, too much or too little of it reduces our ability to function and hinders how well we adapt to new situations. Although anxiety plays an important role in our survival, there's more to learn and know about it, especially when it starts to create problems in our lives and relationships.

For the sole purpose of survival, people throughout history have dealt with their anxiety by coming together. In the Stone Age, cavemen hunted as a team, which helped them become fierce hunters with sophisticated tools. They lived in close-knit family groups, which allowed them to evolve. They took turns making sure the fire kept burning; and, over time, their ability to kill larger animals as a team allowed them to eat the meat quickly, then go out and get some more food before it went bad. Survival anxiety and close-knit communal living came into play at the same time in our evolution. As Jeffrey Miller explains in his book, *The Anxious Organization*, "Survival has always been an anxious business, and forming organizations is one thing humans do and always have done."

In modern times, most of us aren't worried about where our next meal will come from or whether we'll be eaten—that is, unless you frequently hike in rural areas or you've watched Hannibal Lecter one too many times. These days, we're less concerned with merely surviving and more focused on the quality and meaning of our lives. All of us are part of a larger living system; our families, workplaces, communities, and even our solar system are living systems. We seek out a sense of community, rely on our family and friends, and gravitate towards intimacy and connection. This begs the questions: Are we sticking together merely for survival, or has it become more than that, as we've evolved over time? How has our sense of community and togetherness become a resource to help us manage and ease our anxiety throughout history? And, how has it played a part in making us more anxious than ever before now?

We need human connection and the bonds of relationships; however, we also need our individuality. Many of us like to be affiliated with some type of community, whether it's our religion, country of origin, or ethnic group, however, thinking of ourselves as merely part of a herd doesn't sit well with us either. We want to be part of something bigger than ourselves, while also leaving our own unique mark on the world. We want to live with purpose and meaning. Since we no longer need to constantly worry about our survival, we're able to be more aware of our higher-level human needs. What this means is that these days, *a threat to our purpose, value, or sense of meaning can bring about just as much anxiety as a threat to our survival.*

I just gave you a whole lot to think about. I bet you never looked at anxiety that way before. Until now, you maybe just saw it as that thing stopping you from doing what you really want to do in your life; that annoying fly you have to constantly swat away. And maybe it's still that for you. Maybe thinking about the origins of anxiety just makes you more anxious. That's okay with me. I'm not concerned about you being less anxious in the short term, as harsh as that might sound. I'm more focused on offering you a different perspective of anxiety, that will let you manage it in new ways and come up with real and effective solutions, rather than simply trying to avoid or get rid of it. Trust me, I'm speaking from experience. Shifting my perspective about anxiety changed everything for me. I tried everything under the sun to avoid being anxious. I worked out like crazy, avoided people and situations that made me nervous, and people-pleased to exhaustion. But none of it worked. I'm assuming that, since you're reading this book, you know what I'm talking about.

We all have different reasons for experiencing anxiety; but at the core, the process of anxiety is the same—and it's all too predictable. When we were constantly concerned with our actual survival, anxiety moved us to form communities, helping us cope more effectively with whatever was threatening us; however, in modern times, the people we've joined with can pose different types of threats. Ironically, although we tend to feel threatened when our community is in danger, we're also susceptible to being threatened by our community.

We can see this process play out in nature. Animals travel and live in groups to survive; they're so close, in fact, that the group operates as one living individual. When a member of the herd, mass, flock or pack is in danger, the entire group becomes anxious. For example, schools protect fish from their predators. It's just like the lecture I give my daughter before she leaves for a field-trip: always stay in your group, because there's safety in numbers. Predators find it far easier to chase and eat a fish that's swimming alone than to snatch one swimming in a huge group. The reverse is also true. Fish can better defend their territory in a group since predators are less likely to attack a school of dozens or hundreds of them.

Animal groups like fish schools, bird flocks, and insect swarms seem to move so synchronously that researchers have long believed them to be leaderless units. For example, video observations of fish schools have shown that when one fish perceives a threat, the entire school instantly picks up on it and swims away from the threat in a certain pattern. Scientists have tried to figure out what transmissions the fish send to alert everyone in the presence of a threat. It's as if they share a special connection that allows them to transmit anxiety throughout the school, letting everyone know to swim away.

We're just like schools of fish. In the context of our families, workplaces, and neighborhoods, anxiety is passed on from one person to the next. For example, if someone in a family is anxious, everyone else in the family gets anxious. How we differ from schools of fish is that we're often unclear where the source of our threats come from, which leaves us in a constant state of anxiety that can sometimes be crippling. As I said before, the less aware we are about our anxiety, the less we understand what's happening to us, the more negatively affected we are by it. The members of our families and communities are all, at a subconscious level, affected by anxiety. Therefore, when anxious, our instincts are on high alert, ready to respond to a threat at any moment. Anxiety, especially chronic anxiety, is such an integral part of our nature that we only perceive it when it starts creating real problems in our lives.

Unlike fish, when we're anxious, we're liable to make some very erratic and unhealthy choices. A school of fish beautifully synchronizes in a swift movement away from a threat, but we aren't so graceful. We tend to make things worse with our anxiously driven natural reactions. Our reactions to anxiety don't usually solve anything. They just cause us to displace our anxiety, instead of addressing the real problem that started it in the first place. Since anxiety is uncomfortable for us, our initial reaction is to get rid of it immediately. However, the things we do in an effort to rid ourselves of anxiety usually just cause us to pass that anxiety onto someone else—most of the time, without realizing it.

For example, let's say you have a bad day at work because your boss yells at you for not being clear in your presentation. You're upset because you know you didn't prepare enough for your presentation. You come home and walk right past your spouse without any acknowledgment. He sees that you're upset about something, but doesn't know the details. Later, he screams at your son for not brushing his teeth before bed. Your child then begins to scream and cry uncontrollably, which is normal for him to do when he gets yelled at. Now you can feel yourself getting more upset and anxious. Without knowing it, your anxiety has spread from you to your spouse, to your son, and back to you again. Everyone in the family is now feeling anxious, and no one is exactly sure why. It's like a subconscious game of hot potato.

Here's another example for you. Let's say your sister, whom we'll call Becky, is really frustrated with your mom. They're engaged in their usual bickering because your mom always calls her to complain about something. Becky calls you to tell you all about her frustrations with your mom, projecting all of her anger onto you, and pressuring you to agree with her and take her side. Your anxiety goes up, so you call your dad to tell him what happened and complain about how Becky always tries to get you involved in her drama with mom. Your dad talks you down from the ledge and you feel better. He now has a migraine and takes two Advil with a glass of wine, then yells at your mom about her constant need to complain. Your mom's anxiety went to Becky, then to you, then to your dad, and all the way back to her again.

When you look at anxiety this way, you can understand that it doesn't just go away, even if you feel relieved for a moment. Instead, it circulates within the relationship system like a football being passed from one person to the next. Everyone's so busy throwing around the anxiety football that the real threat remains ignored, avoided, and overlooked completely. In the first example I gave you, if your work stress and inability to prepare well for presentations aren't addressed, you'll just keep coming home upset, spreading anxiety in your family like an electric current. In the second example, if Becky doesn't work on her relationship with your mom and her inability to set boundaries, she'll keep calling you and passing along the anxiety football. If Becky doesn't make changes, it's up to you to manage your anxiety whenever she tries to bring you in on her problems with your mom. By setting clear boundaries with her, you'll eventually stop picking up the football.

In this book, I'll be presenting a different perspective of anxiety that will help you function more effectively when you're anxious, instead of just passing your anxiety on to the next person. You'll learn to think differently about your anxiety—in a clearer, more rational way—so that instead of passing it around, you'll start tackling the real issues at their core. You'll become knowledgeable about where your chronic anxiety is coming from, how you can better manage it without feeling the need to pass it to someone else, and how you can stop absorbing other people's anxiety as your own. You will understand the nature of anxiety, not only as a part of our physiological survival mechanism but as an intrinsic part of our relational network.

Bowen Family Systems Theory

The ideas I'm sharing about anxiety stem from my work as a psychotherapist and my understanding of Bowen Family Systems Theory. This theory, which was developed by psychiatrist and professor Dr. Murray Bowen, asserts that to live better lives, our journeys should be guided by a reasonable balance between thoughts and feelings. As most of us know, feelings are fleeting, so objective facts tend to be a far superior basis for good decision-making.

Bowen saw the family as an *emotional unit*, indicating that family members are extremely emotionally connected to each other. If we're honest with ourselves, we can see how profoundly our families influence our emotions and actions. *A change in one person sparks a change in how other members of the family system act and feel. Just like the school of fish, we're all subconsciously connected in deep and meaningful ways.*

When I first learned about this way of thinking, it made a lot of sense to me, even though I didn't fully understand it. Over many years of training, I learned to see myself, others, and how we all operate in a new light. Rather than seeing people as merely individuals, I started to see how we're all interrelated—how we're connected and separate at the same time. Looking at anxiety from this perspective means that rather than identifying the problem within one person, or trying to find a single source for the anxiety that's present, we take a look at the connections between members of the emotional unit and see how anxiety is operating there. In this view, nobody's to blame, since everyone affects everyone else. We are all individual pieces of an operating system; each of us plays an important role in our own lives and the lives of others. *Being aware of this, the goal is to manage ourselves more effectively in the face of conflict and see how we're contributing to the situation.*

Even though I've watered this theory down significantly, you might be wondering why you need to know any of this in the first place. It's because, in order to change your behaviors, you first must understand why you're doing what you're doing. You have to trust in the theory and the process. The best way to see if the theory is true is to apply it to your relationship network. For this reason, I'll be offering many activities that give you a chance to apply these ideas in your own life.

It isn't easy to turn your life around and make real and meaningful changes. It helps to develop an unwavering belief in the principles I'll be sharing with you, in order to finally take charge of your life and your anxiety. But you don't even have to take my word for it. This theory is backed by a growing body of empirical research, which I'll be sharing here too. In fact, one concept that I'll discuss in detail in this book, *differentiation of self,* has been proven by research to increase our sense of wellbeing, help us handle stress better, and make us less anxious.

The concept of 'differentiation of self' offers a lot of information about how we can cope more effectively with anxiety. Being well-differentiated means having the ability to think as an individual, while still remaining connected to others. How many times have you been confident about who you are and what you want, only to later find yourself tangled in a relationship with your parent, spouse, or sibling, that leads you to sway your opinion? How many times have you done the opposite of what others expect from you, just to prove that you can do what you want? How many times have you gone with the flow, just to avoid ruffling any feathers? To be well-differentiated is to be emotionally mature and connected to yourself, regardless of who you're in contact with; it means maintaining your individuality while understanding the emotional effect and pull your family has on you.

This book won't teach you about mental illness and how to treat your internal problem. Instead, it will teach you about why you're anxious and how you can be a more solid, more differentiated self in the midst of your most important relationships. And with that knowledge, you'll be able to effectively manage your anxiety for life. Bowen's theory doesn't focus on mental illness, but rather on the challenges of being human in relationships.

Dr. Bowen also observed patterns in the ways human families managed anxiety, which were remarkably similar to the way animals instinctively handle threats towards their groups. He noticed that our relationship problems are often exaggerated when we're anxious, by the way we react to threats within our family or group. For example, let's say a family member brings up a different opinion during a heated political debate. You proclaim that this person has to take the same position as you, otherwise you'll never see eye to eye and your bond will be broken forever. Or let's say your daughter falls and scrapes her knee, and you run frantically to the rescue. From then on, she doesn't react calmly and instead freaks out whenever she falls. Our anxiety-driven reactions to certain situations can be so exaggerated that they often lead to more stress and anxiety. I'll share some more about this, and what you can do about it, in the next chapter.

Acute Versus Chronic Anxiety

It's important to understand that there are two types of anxiety: *acute* and *chronic*. That uneasy feeling you get when you drive in bad weather or prepare to give a big presentation is what's known as acute anxiety. It's the good kind of anxiety I mentioned earlier. The kind we need for our survival. The natural alarm system in our bodies that lets us know we might be in danger. When the bad weather stops and the presentation is over, the acute anxiety subsides. While acute anxiety arises in response to specific causes, chronic anxiety is primarily created within relationships. According to Michael Kerr and Murray Bowen, "Acute anxiety is fed by fear of what is; chronic anxiety is fed by fear of what might be." Worrying is almost always about what *might be*, and depending on how deeply you think into the future, this type of anxiety can feel overwhelming.

Chronic anxiety is what was preprogrammed into us, what we've inherited from our families of origin. We bring that anxiety around with us, and it can make us pretty reactive, leading to bad decisions and unhealthy patterns. With acute anxiety, a stressor—like driving in bad weather, for example—causes our brains to release adrenaline, also known as epinephrine. This hormone increases our heart rate, raises our blood pressure, and causes us to sweat. There are three biological responses that can follow the adrenaline secretion: 1) Fight, 2) Flee, or 3) Freeze. These are our evolutionary go-to moves when a situation that arises makes us anxious. It's the adrenaline that's being released, which allows us, like all other animals, to react when in danger.

For the most part, I'll be addressing only chronic anxiety in this book. This is the anxiety that most of us go see therapists for or take medication to manage. It's the anxiety that we walk around with daily, even when there's no imminent danger in sight. This anxiety comes from our families of origin, and from the anxiety circulating in our families, workplaces, and communities. It causes our brains to secrete corticosteroid hormones, such as cortisol. Researchers are just scratching the surface in their discovery of the many hormones that get released in chronically anxious organisms; however, they've already identified many effects that those hormones have on our bodies. Corticosteroids are anti-allergic and anti-inflammatory; their biological purpose is to heal the body from the cellular damage that happens as a result of chronic anxiety. However, there are other, much less pleasant effects of these hormones being secreted, such as ulcers, infection, high blood pressure, weight retention and possibly even aging in the brain, which can lead to dementia and other health issues that I'll discuss later in the book. For this reason, doctors who are up to date on the latest research will ask their patients about their personal lives and stress levels when they come in with certain health issues.

I know hearing all of this information doesn't make managing your anxiety any easier. I'm not sharing it to make you more anxious. I'm sharing it so you can see that when we ignore or numb our everyday anxiety, our health is impacted in unimaginable ways. It's critically important that we face our chronic anxiety head-on and make the necessary changes in our lives. However, making real changes isn't easy. We must have a bigger goal and purpose in mind and be knowledgeable about the consequences of our patterned reactions to the problems we face. This helps us become more aware of what we're giving our time and energy to. For me, incorporating this awareness has led me to make changes that help me live a healthier life, filled with effective strategies for dealing with and managing chronic anxiety.

I understand and can sympathize if you feel overwhelmed or at a loss. For most of my life, I tried to deny and cut off from anxiety, but it didn't work. Instead, chronic anxiety wreaked havoc on my body. In my early 20s, I was suffering from panic attacks, muscle spasms, stiff neck and shoulders, and daily migraines. I had to get pretty uncomfortable to embark on making changes in my life. Funny enough, I got really upset with my primary doctor when he insinuated that my health issues had to do with stress. "How dare he blame me for my health issues and suggest I play some part in immobilizing my neck?!" I thought. I was mortified and, in the end, angry with myself. However, what I didn't realize was that it wasn't my fault. I was part of a larger system, and my anxiety was manifesting in ways that I had no control over at the time.

Just like it wasn't my fault, it isn't yours. As I've explained here, there's an entire evolutionary, biological, and systemic explanation for all of this. This might have you throwing your hands up saying, "Well, I'm screwed. There isn't anything I can do about this." But, in fact, there's a great deal you can do about it. It starts with you thinking about yourself and your interactions with others in a new way. This book will give you a blueprint for improving your relationships, differentiating yourself, and managing your anxiety, so that you can reach your goals in life. You hold the key to what you want to create for your life. Regardless of the history that stands behind you, and the hormones that live within you, you can still live a good life.

 SUMMARY

Acute anxiety is often appropriate and protective when it is in response to a true threat. When it comes to chronic anxiety, causes are never as simple as they may seem and often related to imagined threats or beliefs. As this chapter emphasized, the experience of distress can be pretty complicated. When viewing anxiety through the lens of Bowen Family Systems Theory, a systemic way of looking at a complex problem, it becomes clear that anxiety isn't just some defect playing out within one person. From this perspective, it's helpful to look not only at the individual, but at the whole family system, when attempting to understand chronic anxiety. When you can see each relationship system that you operate in as a whole, and understand the role you play in it, you tap into a valuable resource that can help you manage your anxiety over time.

ACTIVITY:
OBSERVER OF YOUR OWN LIFE

We're all researchers in our own right, always observing our environments and the people around us, and making judgments and assumptions about why things are the way they are. Why did Jennifer from the office say what she said to me? Why did that jerk cut me off in traffic? Why does my dad have anger issues, and why can't my sister keep friends? Like good researchers, we're constantly coming up with theories to explain why certain situations occurred. However, there's a big difference between making observations about people and situations, and making assumptions about them. Observations come from a more curious and objective place, while judgments and assumptions come from our subjective experiences and prejudices.

For this activity, I'd like you to practice being an observer of your own life, much like a researcher or journalist. Whether you're at a family dinner, at a work meeting, or about to bring up something important and anxiety-provoking to your spouse, practice being an observer, without making assumptions. Watch how anxiety gets transferred from one person to the next; take note of how it spreads like wildfire; pay attention to what it brings up for you. A tightness in the chest? Shoulder pain? Anger? Frustration? An urge to smooth things over? Whatever it is, just observe it. Watch the natural process at work.

Afterward, ask yourself:

1. What did I notice when I was simply observing my own life?
2. How did the anxiety circulate?
3. What is my automatic reaction to others being anxious?

CHAPTER 2

WHY BEING ANXIOUS IS NOT YOUR FAULT

Seeing the difference between reality and what you feel

GOOD NEWS! YOU'RE NOT CRAZY. I know it can sure feel like it when your life is consumed with anxiety, but you aren't. And none of the other people in your life who deal with anxiety are crazy either. As you read in Chapter 1, all living beings are anxious. At its core, anxiety is merely an expression of our instinct to survive. When you're anxious, you're alert. You're ready to react. So, anxiety isn't a dysfunction or birth defect, it's what gives us the push to do something in response to a threat. From this perspective, it becomes clear that anxiety can be considered an asset, necessary for survival. Issues arise however when we have trouble seeing the difference between real and imagined threats. Then we don't apply a helpful response to that threat, usually because we aren't understanding it clearly or accurately. In our daily lives, we encounter many people and situations that our instincts might perceive as a threat. When that happens, we usually react with our emotions, instead of assessing the situation with rational thoughts. When we react to imagined threats from instinct and emotion, we tend to apply a solution that's not useful. Our instinctive response often does "feel better", to reduce our anxiety in the moment, but does nothing to change our level of anxiousness. It is this response that contributes to chronic

15

anxiety. Emotionally-driven actions are often counterproductive; we behave in ways that distract us from being able to clearly see and evaluate the facts and circumstances, blurring our ability to differentiate between real versus imagined threats.

Gabrielle came to see me for therapy because she was feeling distant and disconnected from her parents. As we got to talking, Gabrielle explained that she'd found she could dodge her parents' criticism by simply not talking to them about what was bothering her. She never told them what she really thought, and this contributed to a lack of communication between them. Gabrielle felt threatened by her parents' disapproval of her, so she distanced herself and hid her true feelings from them. Her natural reaction to the perceived threat was to hide; however, that way of managing her anxiety around their disapproval and criticism wasn't giving her the type of connection she truly wanted with them. Was it Gabrielle's fault that she wasn't connected with her parents? No, not necessarily. It's natural to want to distance yourself from people you feel threatened by. However, if her true goal was to feel closer to her parents, she would have to try a different approach—because her approach was only containing and displacing the anxiety, rather than actually addressing and resolving it.

Without us being conscious of it, we all shape the functioning of everyone we're in relationship with, in a continual and reciprocal process. When anxiety and stress are expressed in one person, it reflects the functioning of that person's relationship with another person. You see, we're constantly responding to each other at a very subtle level. If I have to stay away from you by distancing, it means you're important to me and how I feel about myself. *We're all very tuned into each other; so much so, in fact, that we can think of our family as one nervous system. We're so interconnected that our emotional responses get in the way of our ability to have good, solid relationships.* The quality of our relationships depends on how much room there is for each person to maintain their individuality while remaining connected to each other. We can't fully control the stressors in our lives or our natural reactions to them, but we can improve our coping skills by learning how to respond more effectively to these stressors.

Gabrielle wasn't able to maintain a solid sense of herself or stay confident about her decisions in the presence of her parents. Her parents were anxious about her ability to make the right decisions in her life; they tried to offer advice based on their experiences to ease their own anxiety. This had Gabrielle feeling anxious, leading her to dodge any meaningful conversations she might be able to have with them. They were so interconnected, that their emotional responses to each other were keeping them from truly connecting. Because of this very interconnection, any member of the family has the power to change how the family operates, by changing their own responses and behaviors.

When you see that you aren't crazy, and that your family isn't crazy either; when you understand that there's a larger systemic process at work; when you grasp how anxiety gets transmitted, and what makes you feel anxious, then you can decide what you'd like to do about it. In Gabrielle's case, she decided that if she wanted to have a better relationship with her parents, she would need to work on maintaining her authenticity by not editing herself around them. By working on being a self, Gabrielle took steps to manage her anxiety around their criticism and her natural urge to be accepted by them. She worked on developing herself by coping more effectively with the high level of emotions she experienced around her parents. She got more objective about the threat she perceived her parents posed to her wellbeing and sense of value. And all of this allowed her to connect with them more meaningfully over time.

The Pull for Togetherness

No matter how many times you say, "I don't care," or try to distance or cut off from the people in your emotional system—like members of your family—you're still connected to them through what Bowen calls *togetherness fusion.* When we take a closer look at our own families, a lot of us can see that how we react to life is programmed into us by the very people in our families whom we want to run away from most of the time. I know that idea probably makes you feel anxious; I got a bit anxious writing that sentence. If you've had a particularly rough upbringing, you probably want to get as far away as possible from having any type of relationship with the people who hurt you. I get that, completely. But I'm sure that you've also inherited wonderful traits from your family that you wouldn't necessarily want to get rid of either. Your family, like all families, has shaped you in unimaginable ways—some good, while others not so much. However, your family of origin has developed patterns and habits that you now carry on, which are creating stresses and anxiety in your life. These patterns seem so automatic when you're anxious that you aren't sure you can ever truly or meaningfully change them. And although this fact might make you uncomfortable to think about, it can't be ignored.

I'm not telling you all of this so that you can lose hope or feel helpless to break free from the programming of your upbringing. Just like you can reprogram a website, update your phone apps, and fix the broken foundation of an old home, you can make significant changes in your own foundation. But first, you have to be aware of the powers at work in keeping things the same. *You have to be fully aware of how strong the togetherness pull is, not so that you can make a clean break, but so that you can freely dance between the very barriers that constrain you.* To be consciously aware and objective about this pull is to learn more helpful ways to define yourself *within* those relationships, and also understand how the good and bad parts of you got shaped.

Togetherness fusion is the glue that sticks us together. It's the force that pulls you to help your brother hide that body in the trunk or, more commonly, bail your uncle out for the umpteenth time, when he's gambled all of his rent money. This pull isn't all bad; it doesn't always lead us to do stupid things. It's the same pull that has you drive your sister to the hospital when she falls and sprains her ankle, the pull that has you wait in the waiting room while your mom is in surgery, and the one that makes you take care of your children's needs. This pull for togetherness is what makes a family what it is; it's what makes us protect our families with our lives, loving them more than we love ourselves sometimes.

This pull toward togetherness also helps us manage our anxiety in many ways. Feeling close and connected is better than any anxiety medication. When we give up parts of ourselves to care for another, our anxiety melts away. Our urge to be one with the group allows us to be greater than ourselves. When anxiety is high or a crisis hits, families often come together in the most beautiful ways, with each person doing what's best for everyone, not just what serves their selfish needs. Is there anything inherently wrong with togetherness fusion? No, there isn't. But it's important to be aware of how this force of fusion pushes us to create patterns that don't necessarily help us understand or manage our anxiety.

Problems appear when we totally lose ourselves to give in to the demands of other people. It happens, for example, when your family gets more anxious because you want to be more of a self, which is different from what the group expects of you. It also happens when your family wants you to have the same career type, religious views, or political affiliation that they have. In many ways, our togetherness fusion can lead us to be more like our family members then we'd like to be. When we're too fused together, we lose ourselves, just like animals in a herd; and when anxiety kicks in, this need for togetherness gets even stronger. When one family member gets upset, everyone gets upset. The pulling together as a family softens the strain of facing a threat alone, but it creates another issue: additional discomfort in the form of anxiety. So, in this respect, the solution to our anxiety just winds up triggering more anxiety, further adding to our problems.

Our natural ways of dealing with anxiety, like pulling together, are neither good nor bad; they're simply an automatic response to the discomfort. It becomes a problem when it's the only way we deal with and manage our anxiety. Over time, it's easy to see how our anxiety can become chronic and seemingly unsolvable because we've continued applying the same togetherness resolution and getting the same result.

Joseph wanted to go away to college to study creative writing. Most of his family members lived very close to each other, never having left the state of Connecticut, and most of them were lawyers. When there was a family illness or accident, everyone would come together and take turns taking care of the individual in need. They all had the same political and religious beliefs and got along pretty well. That is, until Joseph told his parents that after high school, he was planning on moving to another state for college. That's when the container keeping the family's anxiety broke open, and everything inside it got released. They pleaded and cried, acting like Joseph was breaking their hearts and ripping the family apart. They tried to make him feel guilty and accused him of being a bad son, all in an effort to keep him from leaving. You see, all was fine in the family, and the anxiety was managed, just as long as everyone agreed with each other and worked to meet the demands of the family. But as soon as Joseph wanted to be more of an individual and make a decision that was best for him, his family tried to reel him back in. Though his screaming parents appeared to be angry, underneath it all, they were really just anxious. Their outrage was a cover for the real message: "Be just like us. Be more for us than for yourself. Lose yourself for the purpose of harmonizing the group." Of course, his parents weren't consciously aware of what they were doing. They just knew that their little boy was parting from the group, doing something that they perceived threatened his—and their—safety. What was Joseph to do? How could he leave to follow his dream, believing it would cause his family to fall apart? Was he to stay with the pack to manage everyone's anxiety? Or leap into the unknown to become more of a self? Which is the right path to take to break free from the shackles of anxiety?

How to Get More Objective About Anxiety

Joseph was part of his family, his emotional system, so it was hard for him to see his situation objectively. He was under the impression that his family would fall apart if he went away to college, that it would make him a bad son, and that his parents might never forgive him. When you're consumed by your emotions, all you can see is your own subjective experience. It's a bit like wearing beer goggles; when you're under the influence, you don't see clearly, and everything looks different. It's hard to make important decisions that way, and it's even more difficult to know what it is that you want—especially when the emotions of your family members are pulling you in a different direction. In Joseph's case, faced with his own emotions and the high anxiety of his herd under attack, the most logical response would be to stay home and take up law as a career. However, if Joseph could gain some objectivity by learning more about how anxiety circulates through a family system, seeing how it functions and the part he plays in it, he might just make another choice. He might see that moving away to college, to pursue a career in something he believes he'll enjoy, isn't an actual threat. He might see that he can still maintain a good relationship with his family while pursuing a more solid sense of self— because the two aren't mutually exclusive. He and his family might be a bit more anxious for a period of time, but they can grow and learn from the experience. They don't actually have to stick together, think alike, and do all the same things in order to live anxiety-free lives.

When learning to manage our feelings and our natural instincts about a situation, we can train ourselves to get closer to the truth. Objectively, Joseph isn't a bad son for wanting to go away to college. He isn't the actual cause of the family's anger, and his decision isn't really tearing the family apart. That's anxiety talking. The clearer Joseph can be about that, the easier it becomes for him to make the decision that's best for him—and might actually be good for his family, too.

Differentiation of Self

When we don't develop enough *self*, we become focused on other people. When we focus on others we are not clear about our plan for *self*. In the context of our family of origin, if we don't get clear about ourselves, our primary motivation will be to figure out what our family members—and other people in general, for that matter—want us to do, instead of acting from what we want. The more you differentiate yourself, the more you can be your own person within the togetherness fusion of the group. We are distinct from other species, in that we can be our own person *and* part of a team at the same time. When we develop ourselves, we can respond in ways that allow us to grow as individuals, without impairing the group. In Joseph's case, the inability to be his own person, and his need to fit in with his family, might end in his family infringing upon each other's autonomy and functioning at one another's expense for their entire lives. Joseph's family hangs closely together because they rely completely on each other for emotional support; this keeps them from venturing out and functioning at a higher level.

If Joseph were to develop more of a self, he would enhance his ability to self-regulate and manage his anxiety. This would bring about changes that would allow him to be less reactive to his family members; thus, his need for their approval would decrease, along with his expectations and feelings of distress. Sounds pretty awesome, right? Differentiation of self is all about learning to manage your own part in your relationships with others, instead of trying to manage everyone else's feelings. It means being part of an emotional unit while being able to control your own functioning at the same time. If he were to decide to stay home, Joseph would be reacting to reduce the immediate anxiety, but ensure perpetuation of the level of anxiety that likely has been constant for generations. Adjusting his internal functioning to help keep his family in harmony, which would most likely affect him adversely in the long run. By paying attention to his body, mind, and emotions in relation to his family, over time, he could become capable of balancing his co-occurring needs for togetherness and individuality.

Working toward becoming more highly differentiated is no easy task. You have to be motivated enough to realize your part in the family system and work on the issues yourself. The irony in all of this is that you can't differentiate a self without being in relationship. Learning to manage yourself when you're around the people who bring about stress is what helps the most. It's all about learning to be present with your anxiety *and* with the people in your group, without having to lose yourself in the process. That's a lot harder than it sounds. It's like running into a burning building, swimming toward a shark, or standing in front of an audience, stark naked. It's leaning into your greatest fears and doing what scares the crap out of you. What makes it so scary is that doing this isn't one of our pre-programmed evolutionary moves. When we begin to differentiate, every ounce of our being wants to jet, scream, or freeze and play dead; but, if in those challenging moments, we can face our fears with the greatest weapon of all—a clear mind and unwavering self—it makes all the difference.

So, how do you become more differentiated? And how does this ultimately help your anxiety, considering it also increases it? The work of becoming more differentiated is some of the most important work we can do in our lives. I'll be presenting a lot of information in this book; however, this concept is one of the most essential to understand and work toward. This is where the real change happens. The calmer we learn to be, even in the midst of our most anxiety-provoking relationships, the more we can tap into the power of clear thinking and decision-making. As Michael E. Kerr, M.D. and Murray Bowen, M.D. say in *Family Evolution*,

> "... differentiation exists in a person who has fully resolved the emotional attachment in his family. He has attained complete emotional maturity in the sense that his self is developed sufficiently that, whenever it is important to do so, he can be an individual in the group. He is responsible for himself and neither fosters nor participates in the irresponsibility of others."

If Joseph can reach a higher level of differentiation of self, he can tell his parents that while he appreciates their concern, he'll still be moving away to college and pursuing a career in creative writing. He won't say it with rage or anger, and he won't express it as a reaction to them. He'll clearly state what he wants for his life, reassuring them that he has no intention of leaving and never coming back. Everyone will hug, his parents will be supportive, and they'll all move on with their day. Do conversations in families ever go that way in real life? Seldomly. But imagine the impact it can make on the family's level of anxiety and reactivity to each other for the conversation to go something like that. Imagine the growth potential that exists for everyone if Joseph can acknowledge his parents' concerns, while staying clear about his desires and plans.

However, considering that Joseph isn't well differentiated, something very different is likely to happen in that situation. He'll either quickly abandon his idea of moving away to college and stay home, or he'll fight with his parents, tell them they can't control his life, and get away from them as soon as he turns 18. In this scenario, Joseph won't have achieved much emotional separation from his parents, leaving him to believe that his only options are to comply with them or make a total break from them. This is because he's incapable of being himself in the presence of his family. So, what is Joseph to do? Given his birth-given level of differentiation, how can he be a self and remain connected to his family at the same time? We'll get to that very soon.

With every concept I present in this book, I'll also talk about how differentiation of self relates to these concepts and what you can do to become more differentiated. I want to be clear that your current level of differentiation isn't your fault. It's something you inherited from your family of origin. The good news is, that if you work on becoming more differentiated, you'll be helping your children, future children, and family at large to become more differentiated as well, thereby reducing the chronic anxiety that's passed on from one generation to the next. Now that you know this, you can't unlearn it. No pressure!

The mere fact that you picked up this book and have read it this far, without throwing it into your bullshit pile, tells me something about you. You aren't starting from zero. You want to learn, grow, and make changes in your life. You're sick and tired of anxiety running the show. You have your own mind, and you want to develop that mind in the face of fear, anxiety, and that scary family member who blows up all the time. I get you, and I'm here with you. So, let's do this.

 SUMMARY

I hope this chapter helped you see that you're not crazy, your family isn't crazy, and your co-workers and friends aren't crazy either. It's not your fault that you're anxious. It doesn't make you a bad or weak person. It just makes you human. We all experience a strong pull for togetherness and individuality that, in some instances, may help ease our anxiety while in others making us feel more anxious. When we're inside the emotional vortex of our family and friends, it's hard to see clearly. We're more likely to displace blame and create more anxiety than we are to remain calm and help the situation we're facing. If we can see *the difference between reality and what we feel* by becoming more objective, we can increase our level of differentiation, which will increase our chances of experiencing freedom from our herd, while also remaining connected to it. It will render us less likely to absorb the anxiety of others, giving us the opportunity to learn how to manage our own anxiety, without having to take on the anxiety of others. And all of this will enhance our ability to live our lives the way we want to.

ACTIVITY:
WRITING BELIEF PAPER

How do you define a self within this tug of war between individuality and togetherness? Well, it helps to first get clear about your goals, values, and guiding principles before you start facing your scariest family members. This helps you to define yourself more clearly, helping you keep your rational brain in play when emotions try to sweep you away in the moment. So, how do you come up with your own guiding principles? Start by writing a *belief paper*, which will help you determine how you want to live your life. Include in this paper what you believe, where those beliefs came from, and what they're based on.

What you write in this paper might lead you to realize that some of your beliefs aren't your own. If this is the case, you'll have to dig a little deeper in order to start living based on your own values, rather than on what other people tell you to value. Once you have that down, think about what you consider non-negotiable. Consider what it takes to build principles that will help you define more of a self. Remember, no one but you can come up with the answers for your own life. I have principles that guide my life, but I don't expect everyone to live by the same values that I do. In fact, one of my guiding principles is to not impose my beliefs and values onto other people, and to be tolerant and accepting of others' beliefs. How very differentiated of me! Some questions that you could ask yourself to help in developing your *belief paper* include:

1. What are some principles that I strongly believe in?

2. Where did these beliefs and principles come from?

3. What theology are my values based on?

4. What do I truly value? What's important to me?

5. What is non-negotiable to me in my relationships?

6. Do my actions fall in line with what I truly believe is right for my life?

7. What do I love unconditionally?

8. What is my number one accomplishment in life?

9. What do I enjoy doing when no one is watching?

10. If there was no such thing as fear or failure, what kind of person would I want to be?

11. If I had $100 million, what would I do?

CHAPTER 3

WHY LIFE STRESSORS AFFECT PEOPLE DIFFERENTLY

The more present anxiety is in a family, the larger the strain on one's ability to adapt in life

I F YOU ACCIDENTALLY BUMP INTO SOMEONE at the grocery store, the person you bump into might say, "No problem. Have a good day;" they might not say anything at all and give you a negative look; or they might be rude and say something like, "Watch where you're going, idiot!" We're all different in how we respond to people, how we take things, and how we deal with day-to-day life. But why? Why do we all react so differently to the same situation? To answer that question, we have to take into consideration each individual's current stressors and family history. Once we start looking at people within their personal context, it's actually pretty easy to see why they react to situations the way they do.

Ever notice how some people have a really hard time in life while others seem to breeze through it enthusiastically? Some people can barely hold themselves together when something bad happens; even when it isn't that serious, they complain and respond with a lot of drama. Others can have their world fall apart, but somehow keep it together and face their problems head-on, with a clear and rational mind. We all know people who keep it together, even in the face of a major tragedy, and others who fall apart at a drop of a dime. So, what allows some people to deal with life situations much better than others? Do they go to a lot of yoga classes or drink some special blend of tea? Do they have a superior outlook on life? Are they stronger than the rest of us? Or are they just born like that? Certainly, some of these variables can either help or hinder our reactions; however, focusing in on a single answer leaves major blind spots that get in the way of understanding the real culprits.

We can say that, due to a number of variables, people react to life stressors in some helpful and not so helpful ways. However, Bowen would argue that our reactions are mostly influenced by the level of chronic anxiety in our family of origin and the amount of stress we're experiencing in our lives at any given time. According to Bowen, if we take a closer look at ourselves and our family histories, we can predict—and possibly change—our behaviors when life throws tough stuff our way. We don't have control over the current level of chronic anxiety in our families, and we often have very little control over the stressors we face; the only thing we can control is how we *respond* to those stressors. That's the one variable we can learn to change, once we have a better understanding of our family history and, of course, our own natural reactions to things. Learning to better respond to situations, people, and life events has a lot to do with becoming more *differentiated*, confident, and comfortable with our ability to overcome obstacles on our own. Once we do that, we start the process of decreasing anxiety in many areas of our lives.

In the last chapter, we spoke about *differentiation of self* and how it relates to a person's level of functioning and emotional maturity. The lower your level of differentiation, the less likely you are to successfully adapt to life stressors. When there's a lot of chronic anxiety in your family, workplace, or community, it's harder for you to adapt when something stressful occurs in your life. If you come from a highly anxious family, your response to stress is more likely to be impaired. If you come from a less anxious family, on the other hand, your tolerance for stress is much greater, and you're able to adapt more easily. I know that doesn't seem very fair. We don't choose the families we're born into, or the curveballs life throws our way. It's hard enough to get through life, but it becomes much harder when you're basically anxious and agitated all the time.

The more anxious we are, the more emotionally reactive we are to the people we come into contact with, and to life in general. Anxiety can be seen as its own category of *emotional reactivity*, given the exaggerated sense of awareness and fear of the future it brings. When we're chronically anxious, we tend to be more aggressive, angry, snappy, and quick to judge. We tend to think the worst of situations and people. Other chronically anxious people might be emotionally reactive in other ways; they might, for example, internalize all those aggressive feelings. Some people let it all out, while others take a more passive response, managing their emotional reactivity by stuffing down their feelings instead of releasing them. Both types of people are chronically anxious, but they manage their emotional reactivity in different ways. One isn't necessarily better than the other, and both reactions are problematic in their own ways. Despite reducing the feelings of anxiety in the moment, neither approach is useful in solving the actual problem of chronic anxiety, and neither will help you become more differentiated; they're just ways to release or push away the anxious feelings.

Let's look at an example to see how this works. Let's say Jonathan has been waiting in line at the DMV for 30 minutes, when someone cuts in front of him. He yells and screams, calling the person a jerk, and telling him he better go to the back of the line before they have a real problem. The assumption driving Jonathan's reaction is that this person is selfish and inconsiderate, trying to cut the line on purpose. Now let's say Jaime has also been waiting at the DMV for 30 minutes. Someone also cuts him in line, and he gets upset—not only because it's unfair, but because this person has made him have to wait even longer. However, Jaime decides not to say anything in order to keep the peace and avoid embarrassing himself in public. Jaime assumes that if he voices his frustration, he'll get yelled at by the person who cut in front of him. Both Jonathan and Jaime are reacting emotionally to the situation, but they're handling it in very different ways.

Now, let's look at Jeff, who also happened to be cut in line after waiting for 30 minutes at the DMV. He figures the person must not have seen the line or wasn't aware of the rules, so he calmly tells him, "Excuse me. I see that you just got here. The line actually begins over there. All of us have been here for 30 minutes already." He doesn't get aggressive but also doesn't choose to ignore the situation based on his emotional reactivity and fear. He doesn't make negative assumptions about what will happen if he speaks up. Instead, he looks at the facts and then states them clearly, not worrying so much about the outcome. Jeff's response to the situation—unlike Jonathan and Jaime's—is a good way to avoid creating more anxiety in his life. Obviously, people don't often tend to respond that way. So, how do we get to be more like Jeff? To answer this question, let's take a look at the individual variations of anxiety and how they contribute to chronic anxiety.

Anxiety Variations

Our level of anxiety within ourselves and our families, naturally changes over time. However, we do maintain a general range of chronic anxiety, within ourselves and our families, that corresponds with our basic level of differentiation. ***Basically, the lower*** *your level of differentiation, the higher your level of chronic anxiety is likely to be throughout your life.* Bowen proposes that your chronic anxiety levels don't have to do with external stressors, so much as with what you learned in your most crucial developmental stages, and how you carry that with you throughout your life. "This learning occurs on several levels, ranging from the seemingly osmotic absorption of parental anxieties to the incorporations of subjectively determined attitudes that create anxiety, such as low self-esteem" (Michael Kerr, MD & Murray Bowen, MD, Family Evolution).

Every family has its own average level of chronic anxiety, which is the product of the emotional structure within each family member, and the ways in which all family members impact each other. The less differentiated the members of a family, the more reactive they are to each other, and the more blinded they become by their own subjective perspective. Members of these kinds of families depend on each other for their functioning, and this dependence spreads chronic anxiety through the family system, leading individual family members to be more reactive and less clear in their thinking.

Because our families of origin vary in their levels of differentiation and chronic anxiety, we all differ widely in how we respond to stressors, life events, random strangers, and family members. Imagine that you were preprogrammed to believe that you're unworthy because of your social status or gender. This idea, that you're inferior on the basis of some aspect of who you are, will create anxiety in your life. Now imagine that you've adopted this attitude as your own, based on years of associating with a certain member of your family. Repeated interactions with this person have led you to develop a perception of yourself as unworthy, and because of this, you're now susceptible to a lot more difficulties. The likelihood is, you won't have enough faith in your own abilities to face struggles head-on; you might look to others to help you, creating more dependence and anxiety in your life.

You also might be wondering why siblings—people raised in the very same family—vary so much in how they respond and react to stress. It's because siblings don't all have the same level of chronic anxiety, mainly because children from the same family don't emotionally separate from their parents to the same degree. The sibling who is the most engaged with the emotional problems of their family is the one who separates the least. That child, who tends to be the most dependent on their parents, typically displays the most chronic anxiety. That child is also the most likely to display symptoms related to chronic anxiety. The sibling who is able to separate the most and rely on their parents the least usually has the least amount of anxiety.

Let's look at an example of how this plays out in families. Heather graduated from law school, moved out of her family's house at 18, always maintained serious relationships, and was seen as the golden child. She made friends pretty easily and could always be found making plans or studying in the library. Her brother, Brandon, seemed very different from her. He stayed home for college, wasn't very social and had never been in a serious relationship. He spent most of his time at home playing videogames, and his closest relationship was with his mother. Heather and Brandon's parents didn't have the best marriage. Heather was focused on her own life, therefore she was able to avoid being consumed by her parent's relationship. But Brandon was frequently a sounding board for his mother's grievances about his father. He felt an intense urge to be his mother's confidante, and he absorbed the majority of the family's anxiety while Heather, absorbed very little of it.

Because of the role Brandon played in his family, he was a lot more anxious than Heather in his day-to-day life. He had trouble maintaining jobs, had low energy, and was a chronic overeater. Heather maintained a successful career, stayed healthy, and was pretty energetic. Brandon was not only the most involved in his family's emotional problems, he was also dependent on his parents, both financially and emotionally. He was never able to launch his own life, like his sister did, and he was held captive by the level of chronic anxiety in his family for most of his life.

All of this doesn't sound fair to me, and I'm sure it doesn't to you, either—especially if you're the one who absorbs most of the anxiety in your own family. I held that place in my family for most of my young life, and some days, I'm shocked that I was able to make the changes I've made. Although all of this can be discouraging, if you're that sibling who has absorbed the most anxiety in your family, it can also be freeing to know that you are not the problem and that there's a way to change your role in your family.

On the surface, it might seem like Brandon is lazy, unmotivated, and has a lot of personal issues. However, upon closer observation of his family and its functioning, it's clear to see why Brandon was running on empty; he was taking on the anxiety of his family. This left him with chronic anxiety that led him to dodge life's responsibilities, give up on close personal relationships, and manage his emotions with food. Brandon wasn't a bad or lazy kid; but because he was already on overload, there wasn't any energy left for him to create his own life. He adopted his mom's pessimistic stance on romantic relationships and didn't build confidence in his ability to create his own life. So, what is someone like Brandon to do? How can he keep the chronic anxiety of his family from controlling his life? For starters, he has to find a way to grow away from his family while still staying in contact with them, learning to be on his own and assume responsibility for his own life.

Level of Differentiation and Chronic Anxiety

Now that you have a better understanding of how chronic anxiety works within a family system and why all of us might respond to life and life's stressors in different ways, it's important to get clear about the relationship between differentiation of self and chronic anxiety. If chronic anxiety increases as our level of differentiation decreases, how can we become more differentiated—especially if we find ourselves in Brandon's position? How can we create a personal identity and become more of a *self*, separate from our family, if we're highly dependent on them?

First, it's important to understand that the less capable we are of emotionally separating ourselves from our family, the more anxious we'll be about forming our own lives. Some people, like Brandon, are too anxious to leave home; others appear to have grown up by cutting off from their families. However, in both cases, there's a certain degree of anxiety about being responsible. People who are consumed and/or cut off from their families share in common that they rely on their families, not themselves, to regulate their emotions. People who stay close to ease their anxiety and people who take off to ease it, tend to be at the same low level of differentiation. *Generally speaking, people who aren't well differentiated don't have much confidence in themselves or in their ability to make decisions for their own lives.* They're susceptible to both taking on the anxiety of others and passing their anxiety on, as well. Many of them try to manage their anxiety by controlling their environment, trying to keep it as calm as possible; what they don't realize is that by doing this, they play a part in maintaining and increasing their anxiety.

When you aren't well-differentiated, it's difficult to distinguish between feelings and facts, which causes your anxiety to reach new heights. Feelings without facts can create overthinking and intense emotions, which constantly feed into each other, creating more anxiety. If you're the type of person who's constantly anxious, you know how easily overthinking can take on a life of its own. **Some common thought patterns that contribute to chronic anxiety are:** *1. Being fearful of living in uncertainty, 2. Always anticipating the worst-case scenarios, 3. Replaying what others might think of you, 4. Wondering if others accept you, 5. Worrying about what you should be doing, 6. Feeling unworthy, 7. Getting overwhelmed by responsibility, and 8. Not being able to accept the past.*

For example, when we wonder if others accept us, we rely on them to tell us who we are; we depend on them for our worth. The more concerned we become with whether or not we're living life on a certain timeline or in the way we're supposed to live it, the more we overthink about the future. *Being overly concerned with what others think, or believing that life needs to go a certain way, is a product of chronic anxiety. This creates an environment in which overthinking and fear can thrive, eventually taking control of your thoughts and decisions.*

I can't help but wonder, is overthinking really thinking at all, or is it just going around in circles? If we've been living in an environment where anxiety thrives, what can we do about it? What if we don't feel confident in our abilities? What if we take on others' negative ideas and thoughts as our own? How can we stop fearing the future, worrying about everything, always hesitating to take the next step? What can we do in order to be less anxious? Simply stated, we become more differentiated by creating confidence in ourselves and our ability to manage our lives and our most difficult relationships. We stop avoiding people or becoming highly anxious at the thought of seeing others. When we build a reasonable level of confidence in ourselves, we develop more tolerance for others, even if they see life differently than we do, and we don't worry as much about what they might think of us. This allows us to have more control over ourselves, even when we're in contact with people who make us feel anxious.

Imagine a world where instead of directing our energy towards avoiding others, trying to change others, or overthinking about how others see us, we directed it towards changing how we see ourselves. Imagine a world where you don't need others to accept you so you can feel good about yourself, but instead feel certain about who you are, regardless of the views of others. In this world, you'll easily find a sense of freedom that will allow you to manage anxiety, instead of it managing you.

Breaking Free from Chronic Anxiety by Becoming More of a Self

Picture that everywhere you go, you walk on eggshells. You censor each thought, editing your words carefully. You overthink your every move, questioning yourself over and over again. Somehow, your interactions with others never go smoothly, and your conversations always seem to take more effort than they should. If you're chronically anxious, you know this pattern all too well. It's hard to be yourself, to be confident in who you are, when you're constantly worried about how other people will perceive what you say and do. *When your fear of what others think is stronger than your desire to bring who you are and what you think to the surface, life becomes a whole lot tougher.*

It's understandable and commendable to care about others and be mindful of how you treat the people you care about. But it becomes an issue when your sensitivity to what others want pushes you to suppress what *you* truly want. Do you find it intolerable to hurt someone you love, even if it's unintentional? Do you experience shame, guilt, or concerns about being a bad person for speaking up? As a result, do you avoid saying what's on your mind and push away your own feelings? If you answered yes to any of these questions, you're probably suppressing *yourself.* As

I've been saying in this chapter, doing this is a surefire way to create chronic anxiety in your life. And it isn't very good for your relationships, either.

Debra came to therapy feeling anxious in her daily life, which she attributed to her marriage. She didn't feel like she could be herself around her husband, Jonathan. On the rare occasion when she would tell him what she wanted, Jonathan would get upset if it didn't align with what he wanted, and told her that she made him feel distant and unloved. She took this personally and began to believe that his hurt feelings were all her fault. It was common for her to be the one to apologize, even when she really didn't do anything wrong. This way of thinking spilled into many of Debra's other relationships, which resulted in her keeping her true thoughts and feelings to herself. Debra experienced chronic anxiety; she tiptoed around her husband's feelings, later realizing that she couldn't live that way forever. *Debra began to see that after much thought and reflection, she knew she needed to work on her inability to tolerate hurting other people's feelings.*

While Jonathan might have been more sensitive to feeling hurt, Debra's unwillingness to express herself, in fear that she would hurt him, also contributed to their relationship's difficulties. When I gathered more details from Debra, I realized that in most of her relationships, she struggled with worrying more about how she affected others than about her own feelings. Debra had never considered that we all unintentionally hurt people, even those we love. She couldn't wrap her head around the idea that it's impossible to be in a relationship with someone without hurting them at some point. She chose to suppress her true feelings and thoughts to avoid seeing someone she loved in discomfort.

As we spoke some more, I got curious about what made it so hard for Debra to consider that something she said or did might have the unintended consequence of hurting someone she cared about. I asked, "Where did the idea come from that it isn't acceptable to hurt someone you love?" We also explored Debra's exaggerated idea that when people feel hurt, they're actually deeply wounded.

Debra brought up that in her relationship with her father, he would get easily hurt by the smallest things. She shared one particular memory of her father yelling at her and telling her how hurt he was when Debra didn't like that he made fish for dinner. He asked how she could fail to appreciate all the time, money, and effort it took him to feed her. *Debra remembered how scared she was when her father was angry, and how much humiliation she felt about not liking the fish he had cooked.* She became angry with herself for not liking fish, and she ate it just to appease him.

Debra began to make the connection between how she was raised and how anxious she was about the prospect of hurting someone's feelings. As a young girl, she wasn't aware that she didn't need to internalize her father's overreactions. She always believed that it was her responsibility to make her father happy, so she worked hard to avoid making him angry. Debra became aware of this, and also began to realize that her automatic reactivity to keep her father happy and avoid his anger led her to overlook her own best interest - especially when they didn't align with what she knew her father wanted.

When Debra spoke about forgetting her own needs and voice, she started to see how she was recreating that relationship with Jonathan. Her anxiety about hurting Jonathan whenever their desires didn't align strengthened her belief that she shouldn't voice her opinion. She realized that although Jonathan's reactions weren't as intense as her father's, she was replaying the same patterns with him. *Ultimately, she came to recognize that she isn't responsible for other people's feelings, that it isn't wrong for her to speak up about what she wants, and that she always*

has the responsibility to use her own voice. Once she became aware of all of this, she started working on breaking free from her pattern of absorbing other people's anxiety.

By working on becoming more comfortable expressing her own thoughts and feelings, and then dealing with the impact this had on the people around her, Debra was able to bring her*self* to life. When this happened, her chronic anxiety slowly started to subside. She became better at dealing with conflict, and she began to worry much less about being a bad person. She gained confidence in herself and her ability to speak her mind, no longer believing that she was to blame for others' reactions.

When we become anxious about the effect we have on others, and we silence ourselves or alter our behavior to make sure we don't hurt anyone's feelings, we operate as a non-self, indicating that we haven't yet developed much of a self. This is not only an indicator that we aren't well-differentiated but also a major contributor to chronic anxiety. *If we can become more at ease about how we affect others, realizing that we're our most powerful when we speak our truth, instead of trying to control the feelings of others, we can nourish the development of our selves.* Debra's case offers one example of how chronic anxiety from our families of origin gets played out in our lives and future relationships. Like most of us, Debra's actual level of differentiation was lower than what she would imagine, so she allowed the feelings of others to influence her actions. The idea that she couldn't express her own thinking when it might hurt others' feelings, came from her upbringing. That belief, along with her lacking sense of self, was a big source of anxiety in her life. By taking a look at her history and better understanding the part she played in an anxious family system, she was able to make real and meaningful changes.

SUMMARY

There are many variables that determine how life stressors affect everyone differently, and the more of them you stack up, the higher your level of chronic anxiety becomes. When you're chronically anxious, your ability to confront life calmly and rationally becomes diminished. How differentiated you are, how competent you are in being a self, how much anxiety you've absorbed from your family, and the type of thinking that perpetuates anxiety in your life, all play a role in how you react to your surroundings. When you look at it this way, isn't it a wonder that any of us manage to function at all in life? No wonder we're so damn anxious all the time!

It's important to note that I don't bring up stuff about the past or about your family so that you'll mull it over and get upset about it; I bring it up so you can understand yourself better and hopefully create a new path—one that allows you to be more of a differentiated self, more confident in your abilities and less reliant on the people around you. You saw in Debra's case how her chronic anxiety developed; you also saw how she was able to gain better control over her anxiety, by responding to the people in her life differently. Yes, she had her basic level of differentiation and chronic anxiety; however, by identifying what made her anxious and how she absorbed the anxiety of others, she was able to make instrumental changes in her life, leaving more room for herself.

If you grew up with anxious parents, you've most likely adopted their worldview, which continues to create anxiety in your life now. However, this is just pre-programming, and you can change that programming. In this chapter, I talked mostly about *learned* behaviors. And this is good news! Just as you learned those behaviors, you can also unlearn them, becoming a more confident and mature self. Through knowledge and awareness of yourself and your anxiety, you can learn to make thoughtful choices, not just pre-programmed ones.

ACTIVITY:
ACCESS YOUR RATIONAL MIND

As I said earlier in this chapter, we become more *differentiated* by creating competence in ourselves and our ability to manage our relationships—even the most difficult ones. When we aren't caught up in worrying about what other people think of us, we're able to have more control over ourselves, even when we're around people who make us feel anxious. For this activity, work on being more of a competent self, especially when a situation or person triggers you. The objective of this activity is *to help you slow down and access your clear mind when you experience stressors in your life.* This helps you create the necessary separation to choose how you want to think about the situation, instead of reacting to it in pre-programmed ways. You can practice this activity by thinking of a past event that triggered you to respond in a way you aren't proud of.

1. Choose a situation, person, or type of interaction that triggered a reactive response from you.

2. Describe your judgment and thought process of the situation or person at the time.

3. Describe your immediate feelings about the situation or person.

4. Describe your thoughts about it now, keeping in mind everything you've learned about anxiety so far.

5. Describe looking back, imagining the situation from the other person's viewpoint and really try to consider their actions without judgment. Can you think about what they may have been up against in their own family or social system?

6. Describe the way you would have liked to respond, given the new perspective you've gained.

7. Then, when thinking it through, verbalize your response about the situation or person to yourself.
    Ask yourself: Would that response have increased or decreased my anxiety at the time? What effect would it have had on my functioning? In what ways did my original response create more anxiety?

CHAPTER 4

THE WAYS WE EASE OUR ANXIETY SOMETIMES BIND US TO IT

Relationships are the most effective way to ease our anxiety in the short-term

WE HAVE MANY WAYS of trying to manage and ease our anxiety in the moment, but the reality is that most of them don't do much to resolve the real source of our anxiety. When we engage in certain behaviors to relax ourselves, we don't tend to realize that our actions aren't just a way of releasing tension, they're also a means of easing our chronic anxiety. The ways we exhibit anxiety, and the ways we choose to ease it, are reflective of our family of origin and of what has worked best for us to manage our anxiety in the short-term. Believe it or not, relationships are the most common means of easing our anxiety. In fact, Bowen calls them our most effective *anxiety binder,* which is a term that refers to the ways anxiety gets managed within individuals and families. Anxiety binders might seem like a helpful way to relieve anxiety, but they actually only serve to keep anxiety alive. To bind something is to tie it so it can't move or escape. This is the purpose anxiety binders serve. Though they might seem to ease our anxiety, they merely keep us tied to the very anxiety and behaviors we want to change.

We all know someone who seems pretty lost unless they have a significant other to help them get their life together. At the beginning of the relationship, this once lost person can start to seem pretty put together; they might even gain a sense of wellbeing and happiness. Watching from the outside, we might assume that this person has finally found that perfect person who will help them keep their life on track. And, while most of us can agree that finding someone who will help you get your life together isn't such a bad thing, relying on a relationship in this way can raise some pretty significant issues in the long-term. That's because getting into a relationship, as a way to bind your anxiety, only serves to keep you *relationship-dependent*; and relationships built on dependency tend to be pretty rocky. ***The more dependent we are on others for how we feel about ourselves, the greater our emotional distresses are, and the more reactive we are to others.***

If you enter a relationship at a pretty low level of differentiation, conflict with your significant other is bound to be pretty intense. This makes sense, doesn't it? When you're deeply emotionally intertwined with another person, it's hard to separate your feelings from theirs, and it's more likely that you'll take things more personally. Being close and connected to someone—especially someone who's helped you lead a better life and makes you feel better about yourself—can feel amazing at first. But this is just another way of looking to another person to manage and regulate your emotions for you. It's not an effective or sustainable method of properly dealing with your anxiety and dependency on others. This is a very important point, since many people use their relationships as a way to bind their anxiety and also encourage others to improve their lives by finding a significant other.

Seeing relationships as anxiety binders offers a pretty different take on love stories like Romeo and Juliet's, doesn't it? It presents a wildly different spin on what relationships mean and why we get into them. Don't get me wrong, we can still find love and connect deeply to others; but if we ignore our personal pain and unresolved issues by diving into the arms of another, we're only binding our anxiety and blinding ourselves to important considerations. It feels natural to depend on others for our wellbeing. We're born into the world vulnerable and depend on our caregivers to keep us alive. Of course, we stay alive through these early years because we have food, shelter, and oxygen; but our survival also critically depends on our caregivers. Having daughters of my own, I see how strong this connection and dependency is. Human connection is essential to us. It's a vital part of life that provides us with a sense of meaning. However, I can't help but wonder, when do our connections with others serve as a way to strengthen us, and when are they merely a crutch that keeps us from blossoming? What's the difference between dependency and true connection?

Claire was raised in an authoritarian household. For most of her life, her parents told her what to do, how to act, who to be friends with, and what to think. When she turned 18 and graduated from high school, she moved out of her family home and traveled to another state, into the arms of a slightly older man. She had spent her entire life anxious to get away from her parents' control, yearning for a life of her own. Finally, she was free to be her own person. For the first time in her life, Claire felt happy and safe. She was away from her parents, in love, and set to be married to a wealthy man. It was as if she had entered a fairy tale. Within 2 years of meeting each other, Claire and her fiancé moved in together, got married, had a child, and were expecting another. But, about 4 years into the marriage, Claire and her husband, Miguel, started having big fights. She was a stay-at-home mom and he was the sole provider for the family. He insisted on having things his way, expecting the house to be cleaned a certain way and dinner to be on the table when he got home every night.

Claire tried her best to make Miguel happy; she was very sensitive to his words and criticisms since her emotions and sense of self were all wrapped up in him. Knowing what we now know about relationships as anxiety binders, this all makes sense.

Claire found herself living in a way that closely modeled the household she grew up in. Over time, she grew increasingly more anxious in her relationship and her home; she felt stuck under the thumb of an authoritarian husband. Claire and Miguel fought all the time, and her anxiety eventually increased to frequent panic attacks. Though she thought she'd made a great decision in leaving her family and marrying a man who could take care of her financially, she had only left one dependent relationship for another. Marrying Miguel eased her anxiety about her family of origin for a few years, but it didn't solve her unresolved issues, her anxiety about feeling controlled, or her emotional reliance on others. Once she became a mother, she felt even more trapped. She couldn't see a way to flee or leave the relationship, and since she wasn't totally clear about what was creating her anxiety, she had her doctor prescribe her medication and she started to drink.

It's no surprise that another common way we ease our anxiety in the moment is with drugs. I think most of us are aware that people use alcohol and legal or illegal drugs—yes, this includes marijuana!—as a means of binding their anxiety. This can ease our anxiety in two ways: within ourselves as individuals and within our families. Claire's instinctual reaction was to cut off from her family—not because she was well-differentiated or independent, but because she was anxious. She couldn't be herself within her dominant and restrictive family of origin. She didn't have the tools or necessary self-confidence to create a life for herself, so she jumped into another kind of dependent relationship. This eased her anxiety about being in her family home and going off on her own. Though her relationship with Miguel was soothing at first, she eventually found herself back in the same position she was in as a child. This time, she couldn't physically flee, since she had children to worry about. So, she fled from her anxious feelings by using medication and drinking.

This process plays out a bit differently for everyone. Claire's is just one example of how someone might jump into a relationship or use medication to bind their anxiety. However, as you can see in Claire's case, her anxiety binders did not resolve her original issues; they didn't help her become her own person. They treated the symptoms temporarily but didn't treat the root of her anxiety. And until we resolve our unresolved stuff from our families of origin, we'll find ourselves in similar situations over and over again, especially when it comes to our relationships. Binding our anxiety just prolongs the process. It contains the anxiety while making us feel a little more comfortable, and it ultimately stalls our urge to make true and meaningful changes, which require us to get uncomfortable. Most of us don't commit to working on ourselves until our relationships are in shambles or our mental and physical health are falling apart.

As I said earlier, relationships and drugs are some of the most popular and effective anxiety binders. Containing our anxiety with drugs, for example, allows us to bind anxiety within ourselves and within our families. Think about it: when a family hyper-focuses on a loved one with a drug problem, those family members can easily ignore or overlook their own issues or potential problems. However, a family member's drug addiction can also be a main source of anxiety for the family, since it threatens the family system. Families cope in many unique ways when one person in the system is identified as the problem. In some families, the addicted person's means of binding his or her anxiety internally might also serve to bind the family's anxiety, too—especially if the way they're doing it seems harmless, such as smoking marijuana or being a serial dater.

When seen this way, you can appreciate that anxiety binders, like addictions, serve a purpose for individuals and families. For example, Tom is always agitated and short-tempered when he gets home from work. This makes his wife, Judy, uneasy—especially when she's been home with the kids all day. Judy worries that Tom will lash out at the children when they're playing too loud, so she encourages Tom to smoke marijuana and have a beer after work, in order to relax after his long workday. She brags to her friends about how marijuana has saved her marriage, telling them how much more tolerable Tom is when he's high. This way of dealing with Tom's outbursts might seem okay for a while; but what happens when life throws more stressors in the family's way? Will Tom need even more beer and marijuana to cope? You see, when our anxiety binders are the only things we rely on to solve our issues, they become part of the problem. If Tom doesn't address his inability to manage himself through stress without lashing out at his family or using drugs, what will he do when his house gets termites or a family member dies?

Anxiety binders rob us of our ability to learn how to properly manage our emotions in stressful situations. In this way, they keep our emotional maturity frozen in time. If Tom continues to blame work for his anger and then uses some type of drug as a way to calm down after work, how will he ever learn to deal with stressful situations without being high? If Judy keeps managing her anxiety around Tom's temper by drugging him, how will she cope when Tom loses it over the curve-balls life throws their way? If we don't learn how to calm ourselves naturally—without lashing out, reaching for drugs, seeking new relationships, or calling someone to vent everything to—how will we learn to be more differentiated? How will we be able to stand on our own two feet if we can't keep it together, without reaching for something to soothe us like a pacifier? No wonder we're so damn anxious. We can't rely on ourselves to keep it together when shit hits the fan!

Unexpected Ways We Express and Manage Anxiety

Below are some additional anxiety binders that you might find surprising:

1. **Eating Disorders.** These can take many forms, such as overeating, bulimia, and anorexia. They serve as both expressions of anxiety and binders of anxiety.

2. **Overachieving.** This can take the form of perfectionism or people-pleasing. Overachieving people are approval seekers; they bind their anxiety through their success and others' acceptance of them.

3. **Underachieving.** People who underachieve are just as relationship-dependent as overachievers; they might bind their anxiety by bringing in others to solve their issues for them, or by not putting any effort into anything. Their guiding thought process might be that if they don't try, they won't fail. They might put a lot of their energy into stopping everyone's persistent efforts to change them.

4. **Focusing on Physical Health and Symptoms.** People who maintain a preoccupation with their health and physical symptoms manage their emotions around a chronic problem by placing all of their attention on their health issues. Family members might soothe their own anxiety by dedicating their lives to helping this chronically symptomatic person.

5. **Hoarding and Overspending.** Some people bind their anxiety by hoarding items they don't need. They might get highly anxious when letting things go, so they hold onto them while accumulating more items. Other people attempt

to manage their anxiety by indulging an impulse to spend and buy things they don't need or can't afford.

6. **Gambling.** Like all anxiety binders, gambling offers a way to escape or contain anxious feelings. People who gamble compulsively as a way of managing their anxiety become consumed and preoccupied with something other than their anxious feelings.

7. **Personality Traits.** Traits such as obsessiveness, workaholism, shyness, indecisiveness, defensiveness, grandiosity, optimism, and pessimism can also be ways that we bind our anxiety. For example, overly pessimistic people can actually improve their sense of wellbeing by lowering their expectations and always assuming the worst. An overly optimistic person might ease their anxiety around difficult issues by constantly being super positive about situations. This can be a way for a person to avoid their problems, by continuing to be optimistic even about bad situations.

8. **Avoiding.** Many people attempt to contain their anxiety by trying to ignore or dismissing things they should be doing, such as going to the doctor or paying necessary bills.

9. **Blaming.** Most of us are guilty of attempting to manage our anxiety by blaming others for our problems. This helps us avoid feeling the anxiety that comes with owning our faults and being accountable for our actions. Some people do the opposite of this by taking on most of the blame; if it's all their fault, they don't have to deal with displeasing others and holding them accountable.

10. **Attacking.** Attacking others is a way of shifting anxiety onto another person. People who bind anxiety this way displace their anxious feelings onto someone else, giving themselves a sense of relief.

11. **Fixing and Getting Overly Involved.** Many people can be counted on to jump in and fix everything and everyone. When they do this, they're often acting from a place of anxiety, involving themselves in problems that aren't theirs, and trying to smooth things over so they won't have to feel uncomfortable.

The higher your levels of anxiety are, the more prominent these behaviors will be. *When a person's level of differentiation is low and the level of chronic anxiety is high, their symptoms will become more prominent and run the show, wreaking additional havoc in their lives.* For example, levels of differentiation and chronic anxiety are what make up the difference between a functional gambler who pays their bills on time but spends most of their money on gambling, and someone who's gambled away everything, steals to gamble, and is in horrible debt.

The list I shared includes just some of the more common ways we bind our anxiety. But, if we observe ourselves, other people, and our surroundings, we can find many more ways that we ease, contain, and express our anxiety in the moment. Recently, I've been noticing that people's beliefs serve as an especially strong and vital anxiety binder. Believing we hold the truth about how the world works, or about what's truly best for us and others, is a strong and powerful force. Everyone, including me, has a huge emotional investment in our beliefs. When those beliefs are threatened, our anxiety rises.

Symptoms that Bind Our Anxiety

What's important to note is that while the symptoms that bind our anxiety may, at first, seem to ease our suffering, they eventually become the problems we focus on. For example, alcohol may initially reduce a person's anxiety; but over time, consistent use of alcohol could lead to alcoholism, which becomes its own problem.

Our culture has trained us to believe that these symptoms are the *sole* problem; however, we must keep in mind that these eventual problems began as honest, albeit destructive, attempts to manage the problem of anxiety. This is why I don't push people to quickly change or stop what they're doing. Instead, I invite them to go slow and take a close look at the bigger picture. We don't know what will happen when people start changing their anxiety binders, and we often don't know how deep their chronic anxiety goes. If we push people to change specific behaviors, without understanding the purpose they serve, we might create more issues or miss the point altogether.

When we, or someone we know, engage in these behaviors, we tend to be judgmental about it. But it's important to remember that people don't choose their symptoms, just like they don't choose the color of their eyes. These are all automatic behaviors. Other people don't choose their "stuff" any more than you choose yours. For example, some of the ways I bind my anxiety include overachieving, people-pleasing, obsessive cleaning and organizing, relationships, and optimism. It took a long time for me to recognize those as anxiety binders because on the outside, they aren't such bad problems to have. To the outside world, I looked pretty put together, but anyone who's anxious or displays these behaviors knows all too well what was really lurking beneath the surface. Even after becoming aware that I was doing these things to bind my anxiety, I wasn't able to stop them overnight. And not just because they were difficult to change, but because other people resisted my efforts to do so. For example, when I tried changing my people-pleasing and overachieving behaviors, I got a lot of pushback from people, which resulted in consequences that could have reinforced my behavior or intensified my symptoms.

I never wanted to approach my anxiety binders with an insistence upon getting rid of them; I simply wanted to understand what they were, what purpose they served, and where they came from. To achieve this, I took on the task of observing myself and the things I would do to manage my anxiety. I looked at the times when my behaviors got in my way, and times when they were necessary. I'm sharing this information about my own journey in the hopes of helping you gain a better understanding of yourself and your behaviors, so that you, too, can see what you're doing that keeps anxiety present in your life. Once you're aware of this, real change can begin. Greater awareness can lead to more intentional efforts, rather than automatic actions. However, adopting this new perspective takes a lot of time and effort. It helps to be accepting and nonjudgmental with yourself in the process of examining your anxiety binders; they aren't your fault, after all.

If reading all of this calls to mind a certain family member whom you'd like to see make changes, keep in mind that all any of us can really do is commit to making improvements in our own lives, and work on increasing our personal level of differentiation. Believe it or not, these efforts wind up being what truly helps other people deal more effectively with their anxiety. By clearly seeing anxiety binders for what they are, we can understand symptoms in their proper context; make true, long-lasting changes; and make that important shift from automatic to intentional. Throughout this book, I'll be offering alternatives to the usual anxiety binders, in order to help release you from your anxiety. In the activity at the end of this chapter, you'll learn how to watch your anxiety, instead of scrambling to bind it or displace it onto someone else.

Effects of Anxiety on the Body

As I've been saying throughout this chapter, anxiety binders are methods we use to avoid or contain our anxiety, which only serve to keep chronic anxiety alive in your life. When we contain our feelings of anxiety, we may partake in harmful behaviors, we also can manifest physical symptoms. If your anxiety has contributed to physical symptoms or medical problems, you're probably very uncomfortable and confused. You might also feel like you're going crazy, or wonder if you're making it all up. However, even though I know it can feel that way, I want you to know that you're not crazy. Anxiety has many known effects on the body that are very real. They aren't all in your head!

Being able to recognize the physical symptoms of anxiety is important. There are many physical manifestations of anxiety that you may notice when you're experiencing situational anxiety or are in the midst of a panic attack. However, many physical symptoms can appear even when you don't think you have a reason to be anxious, and they can have a lasting impact on your overall health.

Headache

It's common for people with anxiety to experience frequent headaches. These can come on during particularly anxiety-provoking situations, or as a result of chronic stress in the body. Stress headaches, also known as tension headaches, come in many different forms. People who experience them complain of feeling like a rubber band is wrapped tightly around their head. It might also feel like tightness in the neck and shoulders, or pain that radiates from the base of the skull, typically affecting both sides of the head. Tension headaches account for nearly 90% of all headaches.

Nausea

Many chronically anxious people experience nausea, which can come right after eating, when looking at food, or in particular anxiety-provoking situations. Nausea that persists and gets worse with spicy or acidic foods and beverages is reflective of a buildup of acid in the stomach, which can cause extreme discomfort and result in lasting digestive issues.

Frequent Urination or Diarrhea

Some chronically anxious people experience frequent urination or diarrhea, which is one of the body's ways of reacting to stress. Anxiety creates a build-up of cortisol, which can cause irregularities in the bowels or urinary tract. In some cases, reducing caffeine intake can help alleviate some of these symptoms.

Rapid Heartbeat

Many anxious people report a rapid heart rate or the sensation that their heart is pounding outside of their chest during high-anxiety moments or panic attacks. This is a common physical symptom of anxiety, which results in an increased risk of heart disease and certain heart conditions.

Chest Pain

Some people experience chest pain when they're acutely anxious or suffering from a panic attack. This pain can be so severe that people who suffer from it commonly believe they're having a heart attack.

Shortness of Breath

Many people with anxiety discover that they have a hard time breathing when they're highly anxious. Their breathing may be shallow and rapid, and some people may even hyperventilate. That's why it's recommended for people experiencing these symptoms of anxiety to practice taking deep breaths, as much as possible, to slow down their breathing. I address deep breathing in more detail in Chapter 9.

Dizziness or Lightheadedness

As a result of the rapid heart rate and shortness of breath that many anxious people experience, they might also feel dizziness or lightheadedness in high-anxiety situations, or in the midst of a panic attack. The number one recommendation for relieving these sensations is to sit down immediately and remain seated until equilibrium is restored. Trying to fight through the anxiety while standing up could lead to fainting or falling.

Tremors or Twitches

Tremors or twitches are common in people with chronic anxiety. Some manifestations of these include twitching feet or fingers, shaking hands, or numbness in the hands and feet. For some people, these symptoms only occur during periods of acute anxiety, while for others they may occur all the time.

Excessive Sweating

Many people experience hot or cold flashes and excessive sweating when they're anxious, even if they try to remain calm. This is one of the many ways the body reacts to stress or fear.

Restlessness

Many people who have anxiety are frequently restless. They're unable to sit still for any length of time and must always be doing something. For example, when sitting in a lecture or meeting, they'll constantly move their feet or drum their fingers on the table. They're likely to find sitting still without fidgeting very difficult, and they may pace often.

Insomnia

Many people who are chronically anxious experience insomnia. At bedtime, their minds stay so focused on things that happened throughout the day, or things that might happen at some point in the future, that they become unable to fall asleep. The higher a person's anxiety, the more likely it is that they'll have trouble sleeping. Insomnia is especially detrimental for people with anxiety, because the less sleep they get, the worse their symptoms of anxiety become, resulting in a vicious cycle.

Fatigue

Some people who have high anxiety frequently experience fatigue, which could be caused by a lack of sleep, or by the body exerting vast amounts of energy during periods of intense anxiety. All of this expended energy can make chronically anxious people feel as though they have nothing left to give.

Weakness

Weakness can be another physical effect of anxiety. Over time, the lack of sleep and increased energy output, which results from anxiety, makes the body become weak. An anxious person might constantly shake their foot when sitting down, but then later feel incapable of walking through the parking lot of the grocery store, because their legs feel weak from all the movement.

Painful Physical Symptoms

Studies have found that several painful physical symptoms, often with no known medical cause, can be associated with anxiety. Approximately 45 percent of anxiety patients report experiencing unexplained pain.

Increase of Menopausal Symptoms

Studies have also shown that anxiety can worsen menopausal symptoms among women in pre- or post-menopause. The most common symptom reported by these women is hot flashes. In a group of over 1000 women, 10 percent of them were found to experience increased hot flashes with anxiety.

Impaired Immune System

Research has demonstrated that many people who suffer from anxiety have weakened immune systems, leaving them unable to fight off illnesses, such as colds, flu, and other communicable diseases. When they contract these illnesses, it's much harder for them to recover.

Digestive Issues

Digestive issues can abound for people with chronically high anxiety. Over time, increased stomach acid can lead to acid reflux or stomach ulcers. The build-up of cortisol, combined with extreme stress, can also cause medical conditions, such as irritable bowel syndrome (IBS).

Decreased Libido

Some people with chronically high anxiety can experience a decreased or completely absent desire to have sex, which can put a strain on their intimate relationships.

As you can see, anxiety affects our lives in many ways. It forces us to engage in behaviors that aren't good for us, creates issues in our bodies, and generally makes us feel lousy. I once attended a conference at which the main speaker, a psychotherapist in practice for over 30 years, stated that every person who came into his office was attempting to manage their anxiety, which manifested in different ways for different people. Instead of attempting to "fix" his clients, he simply tried to understand the problem from their perspective, making therapy a research effort rather than a problem-solving adventure. He stated, "The more uptight I am about trying to fix the problem, the worse the client does. The more I take a research stance, the better they do." This holds true for people in general: they do better when they aren't trying so hard to fix their problems but, instead, just get curious about what's going on with them. Be careful not to confuse that with ignoring or being in denial about the issue. Totally ignoring the issue is just as damaging as becoming overly involved in it or trying to fix it. Think about it, when you're drinking, using a medication, watching too much TV, or overeating, how much of your attempt to stop feeling anxious actually gets in the way of actually solving the anxiety?"

Your limbic system, the personal alarm system living in your brain, is being alerted whenever you're anxious. If you're having trouble managing your emotions to the point of not knowing if there's real danger, you're likely to experience chronic anxiety and rush to the quickest anxiety binder. All of the anxiety binders I've listed are symptoms of being chronically anxious. They're like a check engine light coming on or an alarm sounding; they are letting you know that you are anxious. Don't ignore your anxiety by throwing yourself into more harmful behaviors, without understanding the underlying process of anxiety. That's the seemingly easier, more temporary fix; it's hardly a solution for life. As the saying goes, if you always do what you've always done, you'll always get what you've always gotten. The good news is, when a motivated person makes the decision to focus on his or her *self* and recognize how they contribute to their anxiety and the anxiety of others, things will improve.

SUMMARY

When we're anxious, we become under- or over-involved in others' lives. We use drugs, gamble, overeat, under-eat, shop, or work excessively. We run in the other direction to escape uncomfortable feelings, instead of trying to manage ourselves and our experience. We numb ourselves or cause harm to ourselves, without investigating the real source of our suffering. People are prescribed drugs like Xanax and Klonopin!—which research has shown to be more difficult and dangerous to withdraw from than heroin—to subdue their anxiety, often without any other treatment or further assessment of the problem. Studies have shown that while Xanax reduces anxiety in the first weeks of taking it, a reduced dose, in an effort to stop its use, is associated with a worsening of anxiety by up to 350 percent. Today, estimates suggest that over 50 million prescriptions of Xanax and its generic formulations are filled in the US every year. This is how serious anxiety is and how much it affects people's lives.

There's something about being anxious that pushes people to do things that aren't in their best interest which I can only assume is because it's so damn uncomfortable to be anxious. I get it. If I have a headache, I take an Aleve. But, if those headaches continue, there might be an underlying issue I'm ignoring, and taking Aleve won't really resolve the actual problem. People, who could learn to manage their anxiety in other ways are binding their anxiety instead of dealing with what's really making them anxious. These short-term solutions only make things worse in the long-run. If you truly want to get rid of chronic anxiety, you must become clear about how to manage yourself in stressful situations. You must become more aware of your anxiety binders to know what you could do instead. Once you do this, the symptoms of your anxiety will actually start to reduce their intensity.

ACTIVITY: BECOMING MORE
AWARE OF OUR PROCESS

So, how do we undo what seems so natural to us when we're anxious? We start by becoming more aware of our process, by observing ourselves and changing the way we think. When we examine our *automatic* responses, without immediately trying to change anything, we can assess ourselves and decide for ourselves, whether our responses are helpful or harmful.

For this activity, think about a typical day in your life. As you go through the details, ask yourself these questions: *When do I feel the most anxious, and what is my initial reaction to the anxiety?* Take your time. Close your eyes if you have to. Dive into your experience of a typical day. Is it when you're at the gym, having a drink with friends, outside in nature, driving, at work, or with family? Then ask yourself, *When do I feel the most relaxed?* If it's hard for you to playback a typical day in your mind, start practicing self-awareness, by becoming aware of your internal experiences throughout the day, without judgment. Notice what makes you feel reactive and what seems okay with you. Start to become aware of what you do when you feel uncomfortable or uneasy. Do you reach for a drink, call a friend, or go for a run?

This work is all about looking *within* and getting to know yourself, so you can gain a clearer understanding of how you operate. That way, when you're ready, you can change your behaviors to align more closely with how you'd prefer to respond. Living your life fully aware of yourself and your reactions is freedom at its best.

CHAPTER 5

ANXIETY IN RELATIONSHIPS

*The goal is to know yourself so well that even in your
moments of anxiety, you can make changes
on your own.*

KNOW THAT UP TO THIS POINT, I may have given you the
impression that our emotions, feelings, and natural instincts are
negative since they so often push us to partake in counterproductive behaviors. Maybe I've got you wondering whether it's better
to be an emotionless robot than an emotional human being. I'll
admit, life would certainly be easier if we didn't have emotions.
But I bet it would also be pretty boring. Emotions might compli-
cate things, but they also give us extraordinary things, like art,
poetry, music, romance, the drive to pursue our dreams, and the
ability to form families. Emotions keep us alive and make us *feel*
alive. So why do so many of us suppress and deny our feelings and
emotions, pushing them away without valuing their purpose or
significance? I hypothesize it's because we can't bear the ones that
feel unpleasant. It hurts to have our hearts broken, to feel unloved,
betrayed or be denied something we want. We also make some
bad choices when we're overly emotional, leading us to believe that
our feelings are the problem. However, I often wonder, is it our
negative emotions that push us to make bad choices, or is it our
response to them? What if, instead of denying this natural part of

life, we learned to cope with our feelings more effectively? What if we accepted our feelings, even when they're uncomfortable and unpleasant? I wonder how much of a difference it would make in our lives, and our choices, if we were to acknowledge our feelings, instead of avoiding them.

I'm offering you this perspective of human behavior so that you can better understand yourself and how you operate in your most important relationships. Being more aware of the anxiety that drives your emotions can help you make better choices when your instinctual urges kick in. Instead of aiming for immediate relief, you'll be more equipped to respond intentionally. Making more intentional choices, even when you're uncomfortably anxious, will be far more effective than attempting to deny or diminish anxiety's presence. When you open yourself up to understanding and accepting your emotions as part of life, you free yourself to think of new ways to respond to people, situations, and your own internal experience. Instead of becoming robotic or getting swept away by your emotions, you can learn to discern whether or not certain emotions are helpful under the circumstances. Doing so will help you become more objective and less susceptible to being driven by fear and anxiety. This is why continuously observing yourself and your behaviors is a good way to start making changes. I can't stress enough the importance of self-awareness, which comes from simply paying more attention to your anxiety, emotions, and natural instincts.

Emotions are the source of our reactions and instincts; they're an essential aspect of our human and animal nature. *Our emotions are hardwired into our brains, so trying to deny them is futile.* Many of our emotions are rooted in the patterns we carry with us from childhood. When we repeat, without awareness, certain patterns that have been emotionally etched into us, we're operating from emotions that may have once been helpful but are no longer serving us. For example, if your father was very loud and aggressive before he would hit you with his belt, you might get extremely anxious around people who speak loudly. It's totally appropriate and understandable for a child to be anxious when someone raises their voice; however, that reaction might not be as beneficial for an adult to have, especially if the raised voice poses no real threat. This ineffectual patterned reaction occurs as a function of your brain's emotional inventory, which contains the history of your experience with loud voices and abuse.

This example demonstrates that although emotions are important, they can also lead to many of the difficulties we encounter in our relationships. Without properly assessing your emotions within the context of your past, you might become too emotional to speak up when necessary once someone raises their voice. Such a reaction could make it difficult for you to assert yourself and create boundaries with people who cross the line with you. It could keep you from forming a genuine response because you're too afraid that the other person might get aggressive. Also, if your parental figure was loud and abusive, you yourself may inadvertently become aggressive or loud whenever you want to get your way or assert an opinion. Looking at it from this lens, it becomes clear that some of our natural reactions can hinder our ability to foster genuine and mature relationships. But, if we acknowledge our triggers and patterned reactions, we can find better, more appropriate ways to respond, thus decreasing our anxiety and helping us develop healthier, happier, more harmonious relationships.

Emotions in Relationships

As important as they are, emotions can also create many difficulties in our romantic relationships. Our pre-programmed emotional patterns can prove counterproductive and potentially destructive once we start playing the game of love. Paradoxically, the emotions that lead us to fall in love can be the very same ones that destroy our relationships. I think of the emotional intensity in relationships as a way that *anxiety* is being expressed; whether it comes in the form of anger, frustration, or argumentativeness, this expression of anxiety hinders our ability to connect with our partner. The less differentiated we are when we get into a relationship, the more susceptible we are to become highly reactive to our partner, this happens when we're looking to our partner to complete us. When our romantic relationship serves as a way for us to feel emotionally complete, we become highly sensitive to our partner. Often, we learn from our culture, our family, and our friends that we should find someone who completes us. But when we look for a relationship to complete us, rather than seeing ourselves as complete on our own, we start using our relationship as a way to emotionally regulate ourselves; we rely on it to provide us with the motivation, support, self-esteem, or soothing we might be lacking within ourselves.

As I mentioned in the last chapter, relationships give us a way to manage our anxiety. They give us someone to vent to and unload on after a long and grueling day. They give us someone to turn to for help when we feel helpless. Now, you might be wondering, what's so wrong with this? Why not find a partner who picks up the slack in the areas of your life that aren't so successful? Why not be with someone who can handle all the finances or someone who will bear the full weight of your emotions? Well, the biggest reason is that, over time, looking for someone else to complete you or do the emotional heavy lifting for you will become a primary source of stress in your relationship. Trying to create one full person out of two incomplete ones will not only be ineffective, it will also create more anxiety for both you and your partner. In an effort to manage that anxiety, you'll likely partake in predictable and well-documented relationship patterns that will intensify over time and could lead to the relationship's demise. I know that sounds a bit dramatic. But in just a moment, I'll explain why this could cause a relationship to crumble.

When we don't address our low level of differentiation before entering a relationship, we're likely to feel chronically anxious, without understanding what's causing that anxiety. In an attempt to manage ourselves, we create many familiar patterns that aren't exactly beneficial to our relationship. *Bowen recognized a few of these patterns in particular: conflict, distance, cutoff, over- and under-functioning, and triangling.* For Bowen these are universal patterns that transcend culture, race, and ethnicity. When we engage in these different behaviors, we completely miss the original problem of not being a complete *self* and end up replaying past emotional patterns. In this way, our lack of emotional maturity and inability to resolve issues from the past winds up creating issues in our present relationship. The good news is that in any relationship if at least one person is willing to work on their level of differentiation, their relationship and anxiety will improve. But first, they need to be aware of the relationship patterns getting in the way of improving themselves and their relationship.

The patterns Bowen wrote about are all ways we try to solve the issue of anxiety in our relationship, which ultimately comes from our low level of emotional maturity. By engaging in these patterns, we fail to develop healthier responses to our anxiety. These behaviors, like most of the anxiety binders I described in the last chapter, prevent us from having a full sense of self on our own. The patterns I'm about to describe aren't lasting solutions; they're just a temporary way to relieve the built-up anxiety we feel in our relationship. As I've been explaining, the only true way to reduce the intensity of our anxiety is to become better differentiated and self-regulated.

Conflict

Even though we use conflict as a way to manage relationship anxiety, the anxiety doesn't necessarily have to originate from our romantic relationship. Any kind of anxiety—whether it has to do with our work, our family of origin, our health, or any other aspect of life—can trigger conflict. Think about it: How many times have you found yourself in a fight with your significant other, without knowing how or why it started? It's no secret that conflict is more likely to arise during times of high stress and anxiety. *And once we're in the midst of that conflict with our partner, we tend to display some pretty common behaviors: we become more critical; we blame the other person for the problems we're facing; we project our issues onto the other; we focus outward, instead of on ourselves; we escalate arguments and pick fights.* When our anxiety is particularly high, these behaviors can become so severe that they manifest as abuse.

So, what are you to do when your anxiety is high and you find yourself in conflict with your significant other? Some might suggest that it's time to use I-statements or find a way to fight fair. But personally, I haven't found those techniques to be particularly helpful. *What will help to move you and your partner toward meaningful change is to stop focusing your attention on your partner, and start focusing on yourself. When you can see how you're contributing to the issues in your relationship, you become that much more capable of resolving them.* It takes two anxious and triggered people to create and maintain a fight. So, if you can find *within* yourself a way to remain calm during the turbulence, managing yourself from the impact of your partner's anxiety, you'll be able to overcome and extinguish the conflict in your relationship.

Look, I know how crazy and impossible this probably sounds. As someone who's been married for some time, I know all too well how easy it is for our significant other to tug at all our triggers and insecurities, without even realizing it. However, instead of engaging in the same conflict over and over again—because let's face it, most of our fights are the same thing on repeat—we can make a real effort to stay calm and clear-minded. What do you think would happen if the next time your partner was in high-anxiety conflict mode, you chose a more centered, more thoughtful approach? What kind of difference do you think that would make to your own level of anxiety? The next time your partner is ready for a full-out brawl, it's a great time to work on staying calm and finding the strength to remain present and accountable.

It's easy to get defensive and fight back when faced with an angry and anxious partner. But imagine how powerful it would be if in those moments of intense emotional reactivity, you could take a moment to access your logical brain, which holds the principles and ideas you hold close to you. The likelihood is that a potential fight would quickly turn into a meaningful conversation. The next time you sense a fight brewing with your partner, take a moment to breathe deeply; metaphorically separate yourself from the conflict, and just observe what's happening. When rage starts bubbling up within you, and you feel the urge to attack your partner, pause and take another breath. This will help calm your automatic, emotion-based reaction. Give yourself a bit of time to call in your more objective self.

When we're anxious and upset, we often get overrun by a sense of urgency, which makes us feel like we need to blurt out everything in the moment, or else we'll explode. When your partner comes at you in a heated moment, it can feel like an electrical current moving through you, jolting you into action. But you don't have to indulge those urges. You can see those instincts for what they are and take the time you need to access your more logical self. Then, with the centeredness that affords you, you can

71

reflect on the part you play in the conflict so that you can learn to approach your partner in a reasonable way, even when he or she is anxious or intense.

If you find yourself in a conflictual relationship, there are some questions you can ask yourself to understand what's happening:

1. Is this the type of relationship my parents had?
2. Did I vow to be different from them once I got older?
3. Did I witness a lot of fights growing up?
4. As a child, how did I see the adults in my life resolve conflict?
5. What messages did I receive about conflict in a relationship?

When we find ourselves in similar relationships to the ones we swore we'd never be in, we're presented with an opportunity to explore the impact that our families of origin have had on our ways of being in relationship. This lets us see how our families' emotional patterns have become a part of who we are and how we relate to our significant other. This knowledge isn't for us to use against our parents, blaming them for our past or our current issues. Rather, it's a way of understanding the impact that our family experiences have had on our relationships, which can help us become more objective about the part we play in our current relationship problems. Becoming more differentiated isn't about changing other people or carrying around anger from the past; rather, it's a process of improving our own level of emotional maturity. It's about holding ourselves accountable for our actions, by paying attention to our natural reactions and ways of relating to the people we love. Simply being aware of this and watching the process at work can create a sense of calm. As Roberta M. Gilbert, M.D. says in *Extraordinary Relationships*, "Calm, thoughtful, careful watching can often teach one what is needed to make significant changes in one's own part of the relationship pattern."

Distance

Many of us distance ourselves from our partner without even realizing it, to the point that we don't identify it as a problem. We create physical and emotional distance from our partner, and even distance ourselves from our own feelings. Couples often create distance by seeking space or time apart, seeing it as a way to maintain their individuality. **Some possible ways that this distancing can manifest includes:** *going long periods of time without talking, and arguing whenever you do communicate; overworking; using drugs; spending extreme amounts of time on hobbies; suppressing your feelings when you're upset or anxious; limiting conversation to small-talk; feeling disconnected from loved ones in general, or avoiding emotionally loaded topics.* These ways of distancing can provide some sense of relief, offering a way to collect yourself and gather your thoughts. It might not even seem like an issue in your relationship—that is, until your partner gets jealous or feels ignored and unloved. Over time, engaging in these behaviors without awareness can create irreparable damage to the relationship.

Again, I know I sound a bit dramatic. However, personally, I know about the power of distancing all too well. My go-to move when I'm anxious is to *emotionally distance* myself from other people, as well as from my own feelings about certain situations. I've been told I come across as cold or aloof when I'm in my distancing mode. However, I know that I don't pull this move because I lack feelings; I do it because sometimes my feelings are so extreme that I don't know what to do with them. My emotions used to feel so intense that I believed I had no choice but to deny or create distance from the problems and people I saw as the cause of my emotions. This was especially the case when it came to people whom I perceived as having big emotions and overreactions; around them, I always believed there wasn't any room for how I felt or what I thought. In an effort to get as far away as possible from whoever was hurting me or projecting their own hurt onto me, I pushed away how I felt. I created emotional distance so that I could feel in control of myself and my emotions around other people. Most of the time, I did this subconsciously; and it became so automatic, that for most of my life, I had no idea how I truly felt about pretty much anything.

For many people in a long-term romantic relationship, distancing is a way to make the relationship more tolerable, providing temporary relief from emotional intensity. However, I've found that trying to improve a relationship by distancing isn't particularly effective and the distance creates its own tension. On the outside, a couple engaged in distancing might just look like two individuals with their own respective lives; but because of their distancing behavior, they actually remain emotionally reactive and hyper-focused on each other. Like most of the methods we use to ease our anxiety, distancing provides some temporary relief. But over time, it can actually increase our emotional reactivity towards our partner. When I was able to see that in many of my relationships, especially my marriage, how distancing was a way for me to manage my emotions, I was able to start finding other ways to manage myself through intense emotions. Instead of trying to dodge conflict, I was able to stop avoiding confrontation by bringing up important issues, even if they made me anxious. This helped me build confidence in my ability to think my way through emotionally intense conversations, pushing through my tendency to distance from issues that bothered me.

Cutoff

Most of us have an estranged family member that no one talks to; that person might even be you. Breaking off from significant relationships, also known as cutoff, is pretty common—especially in American families. Divorce and break-ups are the more commonly recognized forms of cutoff, however, they can happen in many different ways. Cutoff comes about as a means of managing the intense anxiety within a relationship or family system. If you look back at least three generations in your family, you'll likely find that multiple people have been cut off from each other. In a family system, this can lead to a pattern of responding to intense feelings that are passed from generation to generation. If your family has a history of cutoff under stressful circumstances, or over issues such as financial strain, divorce, religion, or politics, your immediate reaction when you're upset with someone might be to cut that person out of your life.

In our culture, we're encouraged to cut people out of our lives if they offend us; however, what many people don't understand is that we pay a high price for cutting a family member out of our life. In the short-term, cutoff can relieve relationship anxiety; but over time, it might actually lead to more anxiety and emotional intensity in other relationships. This can explain why many people who seek therapy for anxiety or depression have a history of cutoff in their relationships. At first, cutting someone out of our life can feel like a relief; but it can eventually lead to difficulties coping with other problems in life. It's important to note that given the intensity of a relationship that led to cutoff one should not jump in head first to reverse this pattern, but spend time thinking about the forces that contributed to the pattern, as well as what one wants to accomplish in addressing it, especially in an abusive relationship.

Many people don't connect their current emotional issues with the cutoffs in their life, and this can lead to confusion. As you work on managing your level of anxiety, it will be helpful to also work on thinking about your family history of cutoff by getting curious about it. This will help you gain more objectivity about how the process of cutoff plays a role in your history and current life. Cutoffs can be repaired when we take responsibility for our part in the relationship rift, learn to manage our anxiety around intense relationships, and become more differentiated.

Over- and Under-functioning Reciprocity

Phil Jackson, the former head coach of the Chicago Bulls, understood how doing too much hinders a relationship system from functioning at its best. In his autobiography, Sacred Hoops, he wrote about his effort to convince superstar Michael Jordan to score fewer points in each game. Why would the head coach of a six-time NBA championship team try to get one of his best players to shoot fewer baskets? Well, he happened to have a good understanding of how relationship systems work: When someone over-functions, other members of the system tend to under-function. Over-functioning means taking on other people's responsibilities and not holding them accountable for their participation in the relationship system.

For example, if you're the person in your relationship who takes on most of the responsibilities in your household, you might be the over-functioner. This would depend on whether the amount you do is arrived at thoughtfully or reactively. Over-functioning isn't only about how much you do; it's about doing for another what they could or should be doing for self. It's not only about the division of labor, it's a response to anxiety in the relationship, and how it's managed. When you over-function your partner may be triggered to under-function, doing the bare minimum and not assuming his or her own responsibilities. Just like a basketball team, families, workplaces, and romantic partnerships operate as systems: assemblies of parts that collectively cooperate for a shared purpose. However, a system is not just any group of parts; the parts of a system are connected in such a way that each is influenced by the other, based on what needs to be done. The individual parts of a system can't perform all the tasks alone, as any error or disruption will affect the entire system. Phil Jackson understood that in order for his team to win, every member had to function at a high level. If Michael Jordan, a single part of the team system, functioned at a higher level than his teammates, they would all function at a lower level. Paying attention to this process can allow you to see what part you're playing in the over/under-functioning interaction so that you can make a conscious effort to implement meaningful changes.

Neither the over- nor the under-functioning position is better than the other in a partnership; both are equally emotionally dependent on the relationship. The difference is that the over-functioner is usually more productive. However, this productivity often results in burnout, which happens as a result of performing the tasks of two people. Over-functioners have a tendency to become anxious about under-functioners' lack of enthusiasm and initiative to complete tasks. Many over-functioners believe that if something is going to get done, it's up to them to do it. Of course, we can't know this as a fact, but it is factual that over-functioners operate as though they have to do what they're doing. If you're unsure whether you're the under- or over-functioner in your relationship, this list might help:

As an over-functioner, you're likely to:

- Think you know what's best for the other person
- Worry a lot about the other person
- Give a lot of advice
- Perform tasks for others that they could do for themselves
- Think you're responsible for others' feelings and choices
- Do most of the talking
- Set goals for others that they haven't set for themselves
- Feel burned out

As an under-functioner, you're likely to:

- Be indecisive
- Ask other people's advice when you should think things through on your own
- Ask others to help with things you can do for yourself
- Make irresponsible choices often
- Do most of the listening
- Not have goals for yourself
- Not complete tasks that you start
- Regularly become mentally and/or physically ill
- Easily become addicted to substances

With awareness of this pattern, you can work toward establishing an equal amount of functioning within your relationships. Roberta M. Gilbert points out that "if the over-functioner will stop over-functioning (that is, take responsibility for the self, and only for the self, communicate for the self and only for the self), often the under-functioner will begin to stop under-functioning to a reciprocal degree." The under-functioning partner can also start making changes for the relationship by trying to take on more of his or her own responsibilities. If each person can find a way to take more responsibility for only themselves within the relationship, their relationship anxiety will diminish. Becoming aware of this pattern isn't about assigning blame, it's merely about recognizing our contribution to the relationship pattern, in order to learn how to become more responsible for ourselves.

Triangles

When I first learned about triangles, which is a concept that refers to bringing in a third party to ease our anxiety, I was instantly struck by how automatic this process is for everyone. When we experience conflict in our relationships many of us tend to recruit a third party to help us manage our anxiety. For example, if you're fighting with your partner, you might call a friend to vent; and doing this is likely to ease your frustration. This is just one of many ways that we engage in triangling. **We triangulate whenever we:** *vent to a third party instead of addressing the person we're in conflict with; focus all of our attention on a third party (for example, being completely child-focused and ignoring our spouse); have an affair; become overly interested in other people's problems; or concentrate on everything and everyone other than our partner.*

When we don't know how to manage our anxiety, resolve problems in our relationships, or cope with our lack of differentiation, we tend to triangulate. In order to get out of this pattern, we first have to be aware of it. Then we have to make efforts to tackle issues directly with the person we're in conflict with. Triangulation is just another way of avoiding our partner and the topics that make us feel anxious. As is the case with most anxiety binders, triangles become more prevalent when anxiety is high. People who are triangulated into other people's conflicts usually see themselves as peacekeepers; they tend to take on the anxiety of the people who triangulate them.

─────────────── SUMMARY ───────────────

In our relationships—and our romantic partnerships, especially—we often engage in behaviors that serve to help us avoid the anxiety we feel about our relationship and ourselves. We're masters at avoiding our emotions and partaking in counterproductive methods to distance ourselves from how we feel. Many of us are just repeating patterns that take a lot of energy and leave us feeling stuck and crippled by anxiety. That's why being aware of these relationship patterns is so important. Once we know why we're doing what we're doing and realize that these behaviors don't lead to any progress, we can find the strength to make more intentional choices that will improve our relationships. All people engage in these relationship patterns; even mature families and people engage in all the patterns to some extent. It's when the anxiety gets bound in one pattern that it becomes more problematic for those involved. When it comes to cutoff and abuse, one should tread lightly before taking on the intensity of a face-to-face encounter with the cut-off parties. Confrontation is the last thing someone needs when dealing with such powerful forces.

It's important to remember that the behaviors we engage in to manage our anxiety don't make us bad people; they just make us human. All we can do is become fully aware of the ways that we manage our relationship anxiety. By doing so, we can become more objective about the process at work. With the objectivity that comes with this awareness, we can choose to respond to our partner differently.

ACTIVITY: PATTERNS OF MANAGING RELATIONSHIP ANXIETY

For this activity, reflect on the patterns of managing relationship anxiety that you recognized in yourself while reading this chapter. Then, try to go back three generations in your family, to gather some information that can shed light on the current ways you manage anxiety in your important relationships. If you don't have this information, ask someone in your family who might be able to fill in the blanks for you. Ask yourself and/or your family member(s) the questions below about your grandparents and parents. I understand that your grandparents and/or parents might have been unmarried or single. However, there's still useful information that can be gathered, since the lack of a relationship points to cutoff and distancing.

1. How did they handle disagreements in their relationship?
2. How did they manage stress and anxiety in their relationship? Did they seem to fight a lot? Avoid talking about what bothered them? Lead completely separate lives?
3. Who took care of most of the household responsibilities? (Keep in mind, this could be driven by practicality or thoughtful agreement as well as anxiety)
4. Were they cut off from anyone else in your family? If so, what happened?
5. How did they show love and affection to each other?
6. How did they show love and affection to their children?
7. How was anxiety expressed by each of them?
8. What anxiety binders did they use?
9. What were some stressors or traumas they experienced? How did they cope with them?

CHAPTER 6

CHANGING YOUR FAMILY LEGACY OF TRAUMA

You can't erase the past, but you can change the way you understand and relate to it

Epigenetics Research

THROUGHOUT THIS BOOK, I've discussed many factors that contribute to our chronic anxiety. Another factor I haven't yet mentioned, which can also play a role in our chronic anxiety, is the modification of gene expression known as epigenetics. In fact, recent research in epigenetics offers supporting evidence for Bowen's theory. This research shows that we can carry the burden of anxiety from early life adversity, as well as from our family history. More specifically, these studies show that exposure to environmental difficulties in utero or during our first year of life may have major effects on our internal stress system. *Trauma in the womb or during the first year of life can lock a person's stress system into the "on" position, predisposing that person's body to excessive levels of the stress hormone cortisol, which is secreted by the body during experiences of stress.* For example, an expectant mother experiencing high levels of stress or trauma from an accident, abuse, loss of a loved one, or divorce, may experience biological changes in her body that affect her developing fetus. As researcher and writer Daniel P. Keating stated, "An epigenetic change known as "methylation"—named after methyl, the chemical compound that is responsible—shuts down a key gene that is designed to tell the stress system to turn off when a threat has passed. The result: stress dysregulation (SDR) that leads to an oversupply of the stress hormone cortisol on a constant basis." In other words, when a gene that's supposed to turn our stress response system on or off whenever we face a threat gets set to the "on" position, it becomes difficult for the stress response to turn off. Therefore, when a child has traumatic experiences in the womb or during the first year of life, he or she is likely to become an anxious person. Becoming a more anxious person would depend on the severity, duration, and number of repetitions of the stressor.

When we're experiencing anxiety, we're in a heightened state of sensitivity to our environment, on alert for any potential threat nearby. This heightened sensation leads to feeling constantly anxious, agitated, and overwhelmed. Though extreme stress and trauma early in life aren't the only causes of anxiety, their impact on our lives can't be denied. Interestingly, however, researchers have only recently begun to explore their effects. When tension is high, many young children lash out at others or throw fits. In such a state, their minds are on constant alert, always looking out and never letting their guard down. Children who learn—either in the womb or during the first year of life—that the world isn't a safe place have a stress response that adapts to being on all the time. In the womb, this learning happens most often in extreme situations, when a mother's cortisol level gets high enough that the stress hormone passes into the blood of the fetus. If you think your mother may have experienced a trauma or suffered severe stress while you were in the womb, or if something major happened in your family during your first year of life, I recommend that you read the book *Born Anxious: The Lifelong Impact of Early Life Adversity—And How to Break the Cycle* by Daniel P. Keating. This book tells the story of how stress in early life can fundamentally change the life of a child, making it difficult for that child to learn, make friends, find a spouse, earn a living, and remain healthy. If you worry about your own children, because you experienced a traumatic event during your pregnancy or the first year of parenting, the book can offer valuable tips for helping your children thrive. Though, keep in mind that a single trauma likely wouldn't be enough to make a great difference, unless your level of differentiation was so low that you couldn't be resilient during that time. And, if the parental relationship wasn't good during this period of time then that could be a contributing factor towards an anxious child. If the parental relationship was sufficiently strong the event or events might not have had such significant effects on the child.

Epigenetic research also takes a broad look at the importance of family history and the impact of unresolved issues from our past on our current functioning. *Researchers are finding that we are deeply affected by our family history and that we inherit feelings from our ancestors.* So, if you aren't sure that certain fears and anxiety started with you, it's helpful to take a look at your family history. You might be wondering what the point of that is since we can't change the past. By becoming more aware of our family history of trauma, what we can change is how the past affects our life now.

The latest scientific research supports that traumatic experiences can be passed down through generations. Yes, you read that correctly. It sounds a bit like science fiction, doesn't it? But it's true. Even if the person who suffered the original trauma has died, or the story has been forgotten or kept secret, the memories and feelings of that traumatic event can live on. These emotional legacies are often unseen; yet they're programmed into everything, from gene expression to everyday language, and they play a bigger role in our emotional and physical health than we ever could have imagined.

Epigenetic research explains something groundbreaking: The source of your anxiety isn't necessarily always coming from *you*, but instead from your family history. Which is Bowen's concept of the multi-generational transmission process. Now that we know that trauma can be passed down from generation to generation, it's important to consider how we can break the cycle in our lifetime. Since traumatic events can affect the way we feel and react, interrupting this cycle is vital. That's because traumas, like genes, can only be passed on from generation to generation when they're left unresolved. Below I discuss some of the main points made by Mark Wolynn in his book, *It Didn't Start With You: How Inherited Family Trauma Shapes Who We Are And How To End The Cycle,* which explains epigenetic research in more detail. He also discusses how you can break the cycle if you believe your anxiety derives from trauma in your family lineage.

1. **Trauma that originated in your family history can create negative behaviors and feelings within you, even though you didn't personally experience the trauma.** All of us struggle with anxiety to some extent. We're not talking about DSM-defined clinical anxiety, rather the response of the organism to a perception of threat, real or imagined. Some of us have extreme fears, act out in maladaptive ways, or feel trapped in bad relationships. When we act out or feel anxious, we might think that we're solely to blame. However, unhelpful and stressful behaviors can come about from trauma experienced, directly or indirectly, from our lineage. Traumatic events in our family history, such as a major loss or an act of violence, can affect us to our core. These events not only create extreme stress and fear but can also change our behaviors. Most importantly, if our ancestors weren't able to resolve their symptoms of trauma, they might have suppressed them, resulting in unhealthy behavioral patterns that got passed

down to us. In other words, you might be carrying symptoms of trauma that you didn't personally experience. Severe traumas—like, for example, surviving the Holocaust—can be so powerful that they echo through the family line, affecting future generations who didn't personally experience them.

2. **Personal traumas can be passed on to future generations through genes and behavior.** Even if you don't know much about your parents' or grandparents' past, the lives they lived and the traumas they experienced will have some effect on you. Studies show that past traumas can lead to behavioral patterns that deeply impact family dynamics. Many families hide the effects of painful or traumatic events by never talking about or resolving them. That's why it's so important for us to seek resolution for the effects of trauma in our lives now. If we don't, the future generations of our families could find themselves in the same fierce cycle of inherited traumatic feelings. For example, the death of a child is a traumatic event for anyone. However, if the parents don't deal with the reality of their loss, they'll likely project this trauma on to their next child. As I've been saying, research has shown that thoughts and emotions can alter a person's genetic code or DNA. This means that a person who suffers from trauma might pass "traumatized" genes on to children. According to Stanford University cell biologist Bruce Lipton, emotions like fear or anger can *"biochemically alter the genetic expression of offspring."* Trauma also alters stress hormones, and parents can pass these changes on to their children. Therefore, when it comes to identifying and overcoming anxiety, we must take our family history into consideration.

3. **Resolving parent-child relationships is key in breaking the cycle of trauma.** Whether you like it or not, no one affects who you are and how you feel about yourself as much as your

parents do. Your relationship with your parents shapes who you are as a person. They're the people who gave you life, and the *life force* they instilled in you carries on. There are four ways a parent-child relationship can be disrupted. These are known as the ***Four Unconscious Themes: (1) an overly dependent child-parent relationship; (2) the rejection of a parent; (3) a rift in the relationship with the mother; and (4) trauma inherited from a family member.*** If you suffer from traumatic symptoms or emotional issues, look at your family history and the events of your early childhood; doing so might help explain what's happening in your emotional life today. If you wonder whether you experienced an *interrupted bond,* for instance, explore the events of your mother's pregnancy, whether you might have been adopted, or if you were separated from your mother before you were three years old.

4. **Discover underlying fears or traumas by exploring the language we use to shed light on their true nature.** It's common to be afraid of flying or snakes; however, there are many less common fears that are often rooted in trauma from your personal or ancestral past. We have to be particular with the language we use for describing hidden fears because we often don't have simple words for them. This is especially true when the fear stems from early childhood trauma or inherited trauma. Sigmund Freud wrote about *repetition compulsion,* which occurs when a person unconsciously tries to bring suppressed trauma to the surface through repetitive behavior. According to Mark Wolynn, our memory, or even the absence of memory, can alter our experiences. Therefore, he proposes using *core language* to pinpoint the source of the trouble. For example, one of Wolynn's patients believed that, "The world isn't a safe place. You have to hide who you are. People can hurt you." Those thoughts, the client's *core language,* were

rooted in her great aunt's experience in the Holocaust. Her inherited trauma was controlling her. You can't overcome your fears until you know specifically what they are. Therefore, it helps to start with uncovering your fears by finding your *core complaint*. Wolynn explains that the *core complaint* is a phrase that describes your current fear or phobia, such as "I'm out of control right now and I'm afraid of what I might do." Next, identify your *core sentence*, or the outcome that could result if your fear comes true. It might be something like, "I'll hurt my child" or "My partner will abandon me," for instance. Once you've found your *core complaint* and *core sentence,* you can start to work on the link between your fears and your family's history.

5. **Your deepest fears can help point you toward the source of trauma in your family history.** Our fears and anxieties can guide us to the source of our pain. Instead of trying to run away from our symptoms, we can pay attention to them as a way of uncovering the root of the problem. Wolynn suggests using the *Core Language Approach* to help you create your *Core Language Map,* which is made up of four components: *the Core Complaint, the Core Sentence, the Core Descriptors, and the Core Trauma.* Each component serves as a signpost, pointing to events in your family history that tell you what you fear and why you fear it. Find your *core trauma* by examining your deepest fears and anxieties, and the language you use to describe them. The grandchild of a Holocaust survivor, for instance, had a fear that she was going to "vaporize" and that her body would "incinerate in seconds." Such language indicated that she was affected by a deeply traumatic event in her family's past. When she looked into her family history, she found that her *core trauma* was that her relatives were targeted for extermination as part of the Holocaust during

World War II. You can use the insights you gain from your *Core Language Map* in two ways. The first is through *Bridging Questions* or asking questions around your fear to discover patterns that stem from your family history. If a person is afraid of hurting a child, for example, a *Bridging Question* might be, "Did someone in your family blame themselves for hurting a child?" Or perhaps, "Did anyone in your family feel responsible for a child's death?" The second is to create a *family tree*, which we will be doing in the activity section of this chapter. This is a way to trace your family history back three or four generations, and write any traumatic events next to the name of the family member who experienced them.

6. **Free yourself from inherited trauma by making peace with your past and your family's past.** A problem is a lot easier to solve once it's been identified, so identifying trauma is the first step toward overcoming it. Creating a new visual and verbal language that allows you to communicate with yourself is an important part of the healing process. When you recognize that a relative's trauma is holding you back, you can work on breaking the cycle so that the trauma stops with your generation. To do so, you can use *healing sentences* to help you acknowledge your pain and the pain of people who suffered the original trauma. If you repeat a negative sentence like "I'm a failure" over and over again, you might start to believe it. *Healing sentences* work to instill positive feelings, such as, "Instead of reliving what happened to *you*, I promise to live my life fully." Another might be, "These are not my feelings. I've inherited them from my family." You can also try a *healing action*, such as lighting a candle in memory of someone in your family with whom you've become estranged. A *ceremonial act* could help you find a safe, emotional connection with that person, which serves as an important step toward finding

forgiveness or acceptance. *Healing sentences* can also help you heal your relationship with your parents, which plays a key role in your healing process, especially if your trauma stems from early childhood. Using a *healing sentence* such as "I'll take your love as you give it, not as I expect it" can be helpful, even if your parents are no longer alive. This sentence allows you to accept and forgive your parents' shortcomings. Coming to terms with your struggles, communicating about them using the right language, and accepting other people's struggles, too, are all important parts of healing a relationship.

Overall, it's important to avoid assuming that you're the sole source of your trauma or anxious feelings. Your emotional struggles might have been passed down from relatives, genes, or historical relationships. Along with everything I talk about in this book, you can use the *Core Language Approach* to identify your trauma, find its source, and ultimately overcome it. It's time to break the cycle by coming to terms with your history of trauma so that you don't pass it on to the next generation.

─────────── SUMMARY ───────────

If you think the trauma of a grandparent's experience in the Holocaust, a parent's experience in a war, or an ancestor's escape as a refugee from an unsafe country ended with them, you're mistaken. A growing field of research, called epigenetics, shows that the descendants of trauma survivors have a biological memory of the hardship their relatives endured, through alterations in certain genes and the levels of circulating stress hormones. As Rachel Yehuda—professor of psychiatry and neuroscience at the Icahn School of Medicine, Mount Sinai—explained, "There is evidence that epigenetic changes that are made through stress or adversity can have long-lasting effects that may impact your stress system or sex cells."

From an evolutionary perspective, these transgenerational effects may be important for our survival. "They might prepare subsequent generations for similar conditions because, for example, the stress hormone axis may be already prepared to encounter these environmental conditions," according to Dr. Torsten Klengel, a psychiatrist and research scientist at McLean Hospital, which is affiliated with Harvard Medical School. "But if you don't encounter these conditions, the stress hormone system remains highly active, which can lead to dysregulation of the HPA [the hypothalamic-pituitary-adrenal] axis and could trigger psychiatric disorders and stress-related disorders," such as anxiety and depression. Simply said, being in a continuous state of high alert means your body's fight-or-flight response is constantly accelerating and releasing adrenaline and cortisol, which could be harmful to your body and mind. However, it's important to realize that the effects of this aren't necessarily negative. "You're more sensitive, not necessarily damaged," Yehuda explains. "If you have a parent who has experienced trauma, this may make you more resilient in some ways and more vulnerable in others. When you inherit the effects of trauma, you also may inherit a sensitivity that alerts you to signs of danger earlier and allows you to respond positively in ways that are powerful and effective." She also stated, "We don't want people to think that if something bad happened to your parent, you're doomed. We're dealing with a dynamic biology and we have healing and restorative capacities. We can transform these experiences because our biology helps us adapt. You can get to a good place from a bad place."

ACTIVITY: CREATING A
MULTIGENERATIONAL FAMILY TREE

Create a record of your family history, which is also known as a family tree or genogram. Look back three or four generations, and write down any traumatic events next to the name of the family member(s) who experienced them. A traumatic event might be the early death of a loved one, or a cutoff from the family due to a fight or major traumatic event, such as a genocide. When creating your family genogram, use a square to represent a male family member and a circle to represent a female. Depict nuclear families by drawing a horizontal line connecting the parents—represented by a circle and square—and then drawing a vertical line below for each child, depicting them from left to right to indicate oldest to youngest. Below is an example of a basic family genogram going back three generations.

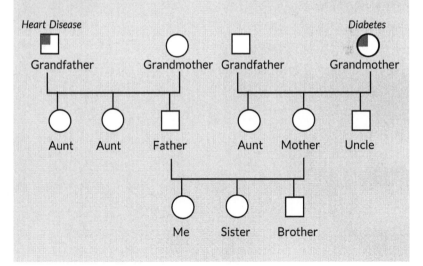

CHAPTER 7

PREDISPOSED TO ANXIETY, DESTINED FOR SELF-RELIANCE

*Instead of dancing around our issues to avoid suffering,
what if we built on our capacity to rely on ourselves?*

I F YOU'VE READ THROUGH ALL THE CHAPTERS thus far, you've received a lot of information, some of which might have left you feeling more anxious. If that's the case, I'm truly sorry and I totally get it. When I first started to expand my knowledge about human behavior and anxiety, it made me more anxious, too. It's hard to take a good look at ourselves, and it's even more difficult to realize that some of the behaviors we might have seen as being positive are actually contributing to our anxiety. That's definitely not easy to digest; it can make you feel like you've been dancing in circles your entire life. I know all about this because I was a hardcore people-pleaser for most of my life; I thought I was doing the right thing by always aiming for others' approval. People-pleasing did help to ward off some of my anxiety around being disapproved of and disappointing others. However, it wasn't actually helpful in resolving why I was anxious.

I lived in constant fear of being disapproved of or criticized, so I worked tirelessly to be perfect. On the rare occasion that I managed to disappoint someone in spite of my best efforts, it killed me. In the long run, people-pleasing did nothing to help me work on my fears. Instead of building confidence in myself or learning how to manage my anxiety around disapproval, I became a walking doormat. Once I recognized this, I knew I had to become more self-confident and learn how to speak my mind and say things that others may not want to hear. That very idea made me anxious, nauseous, and super tense. No wonder I was avoiding disapproval! Just like you, I inherited and learned some behaviors, like pleasing, that were really just attempts to manage my anxiety.

Like I've mentioned before, how you've learned to manage your anxiety isn't your fault; actually, some of your behaviors might have been helpful to you when you were young. When I was young, people-pleasing helped me to feel safe and approved of in my critical home environment; I didn't have the mental capacity to deal with my anxious home in any other way. But now that I'm an adult, I can make the choice to either continue the old patterns that no longer serve me, or make more deliberate choices, as hard and painful as they may be. I committed to learning how to make more deliberate choices because, at the end of the day, I wanted freedom from my anxiety and instinctual behavior patterns. I also wanted what was best for my most important relationships, and the only way I could do that was by defining myself and using my own voice. As it goes when we try to acquire anything worthwhile in life, if there's no pain, there's no gain.

A common theme in all the information I've given you so far is that we're all just trying to manage whatever problems we're facing in the moment, using the tools that were provided for us. However, when we do that, our problems don't really get solved. We muddle through and just cope with life the way we always have. The way our families have for generations before us. Most of us find a way to manage life's challenges without engaging in much deep thought; we simply keep doing what we normally do, even if it isn't working. Instead of solving our challenges, we maintain them; we don't make them worse, but we don't make them any better, either. Life comes together for some time, then falls right back apart again. Eventually, things come back together again, only to fall apart once more. If you think about your life so far, I'm sure it's played out that way. However, if you can become aware of your family patterns, instead of living on repeat, you can consider how you'd prefer to respond, and how you can maintain your sanity while you face those challenges head-on. You can practice managing yourself in uncomfortable situations instead of distancing yourself from them. You can lean in to anxiety, knowing that backing away just creates more of it in the future.

Anxiety is ignited when we don't accept the facts of life and fail to look at our own behaviors. From this perspective, a lot of our misery is self-inflicted. We expect the ideal to overcome the actual, and we expect things or people to be different so we can be happy. One of the tricks to being less anxious is letting the tough stuff happen and allowing life to be difficult sometimes—trusting in the process, and self-managing through the storms. The experiences in your life are trying to show you who you are. It doesn't serve your growth to ignore your discomfort. Instead, lean into the difficult experiences; allow them to be part of your life.

For example, we emotionally distance ourselves from people who are more difficult to deal with, even if they're important to us. When we make a choice to avoid people or situations which might make us uncomfortable, we limit our growth potential. We stay close to people who don't challenge us and avoid situations that seem problematic—the very situations that offer us opportunities to truly grow into ourselves.

Changing Your Perspective

We don't fix anxiety by running away from it; the better way to manage anxiety is by changing our perspective and responding to difficult situations in more helpful ways when they arise. The problem isn't only the counterproductive actions we take when we are anxious, it's the thoughts, feelings, and sense of urgency behind those actions. By changing how you perceive anxiety, you'll create a shift in how you manage it when it rears its ugly head. Bowen's concept of differentiation of self, which explains basic systems understanding of personal growth, will help shift your perspective. Essentially, people who are differentiated have the capacity to think autonomously, while remaining connected to others. Within a systemic understanding of human behavior, the only way to define yourself is within the context of your most important relationships. Systems theory explains the fluctuating ability everyone has to stabilize their emotions and logical brain, balancing their desire to be connected with their desire to be independent.

As you may have noticed, Bowen's theory isn't an easy one to grasp. Throughout this book, I've offered approachable explanations of his ideas to support your understanding of them. Bowen's ideas allowed me to see the world through the perspective of each of my family members, instead of being limited by my own subjective experience. This helped me to start taking other people's actions and mistakes less personally. Seeing the bigger systemic picture moves us beyond finger-pointing and helps us see the relationship forces that set people on their unique life paths. This way of understanding our lives and relationships provides a necessary means of defining ourselves through our relationships.

Research has shown that Bowen's concept of differentiation enhances personal wellbeing, relationship satisfaction, stress management, decision-making, and the ability to cope with life in general. As I've mentioned, Bowen discovered that families manage stress in patterned ways that are remarkably similar to the instinctive ways other species handle threats to their packs. *Bowen theorized that our problems derive from an instinctive reaction to things that might threaten our relationships.* If we gain objectivity about our instinctive processes at work, we can learn to change our responses and make meaningful changes in our lives. When we gain a clearer sense of self, we become less reactive and less in need of attention and approval from others. We gain the ability to self-regulate within the emotional system of our families. When we're willing to be honest about how we relate to people, our lives and relationships benefit tremendously. Looking at the relationship patterns within our family system is a great place to start, as they reveal the problems that get repeated from generation to generation.

If you've ever tried to understand the issues you're currently facing in your life, you might have fallen down the rabbit hole of thinking about how they were influenced by your early life experiences. This might have led you to blame your current hardships on your parents. When you think in simple, cause-and-effect terms, it's easy to blame your parents for just about everything. I mean, they were the ones who raised you, after all, and they might have done some pretty irresponsible things. If you've ever had thoughts like, "I'm needy for love because my parents never showed me affection," "I don't know how to pay my bills because my parents were always bad at managing their money," or "I have a fear of commitment because my parents' marriage didn't work out," you're certainly not alone.

It makes sense to consider how our parents contributed to the issues we face as adults. However, before we place all the blame on them, it's important to consider the position they held in their own families of origin. In other words, it's important to ask, how did their parents shape their paths and lead them to become who they are? What challenges did they and the generations before them face? Your parents were kids once too, and throughout their lives, they've faced issues similar to the ones you face in your life. When you think about your parents in this way, it might invite you to look at the bigger picture, seeing them as humans who also make mistakes. As people who were doing the best, they knew how to do in order to adapt to what life put in their paths.

Most of your parents' reactions towards you have come from unconscious efforts to relieve their own anxiety, not from evil attempts to screw up your childhood and adulthood. Your parents inherited patterns of relating to their loved ones, just as you did. I say that with compassion because I know it's got to be hard to read if you had a particularly difficult upbringing and you've held on to the belief that your life's problems have resulted from how your parents mistreated you. I get it. I felt the same way when I first started learning about these ideas. However, if you open your mind to it, you'll be able to see that there are certain patterns in your family system that you don't have to repeat. This will help you to see what you're up against and what changes need to be made so that your children won't yell at you for messing them up 30 years from now.

Seeing that your current issues go far beyond the responses of your parents, their parents, and the parents before them allows you to understand what's going on with you in a way that won't have you blaming anyone. Knowing that it's up to you to look at the ways your family has done things for generations can help you make important changes and heal. It can lead you to address the things you can change within yourself, instead of blaming others. At some point, we must grow up. We do this when we realize that our parents are flawed and so are we. Once we accept that, we can start to face and resolve our anxiety. When you're willing to look closer, it's almost impossible to avoid seeing a connection between your parents' behavior growing up and your own behavior as an adult. It's all just too patterned and predictable to be ignored.

Building Confidence to Work on Your Anxiety

Building something, working toward our goals, and dealing with what needs to be dealt with in the moment, all contribute to our self-confidence. Confidence can't be given to us, and it isn't something we create by gratifying our urges in the moment. Respect, self-worth, and self-reliance—some of the elements that make up a person's self-confidence—can't be earned through avoidance behaviors, either. When we're anxious, we're more likely to engage in avoidance behaviors and suppress our uncomfortable feelings instead of trying to manage our experiences and ourselves. Avoiding discomfort and sticking to what feels good is a surefire way to stay stuck and stunt your personal development.

People think that the anxiety we experience in distressing situations is a problem. It's not. That feeling of being backed against the wall is an indication that there's a problem. It's the fire alarm, not the actual fire. In other words, as I've been saying throughout the book, anxiety is a symptom, not the actual disease. Anxiety is the sign that lets you know there might be a threat in your environment. It's the signal letting you know that you might need to tune in to what's around or within you.

When we change our perspective to see anxiety as a symptom of a problem, rather than the problem itself, genuine change starts taking place. Instead of seeking to get rid of anxiety immediately, we're able to work with it, be with it, and understand it. If a fire alarm went off in your home, you might first assess the situation, look around, and try to identify the source of the smoke. You might call the fire station for backup if you see an actual fire. But I'm sure you wouldn't just run off and do nothing about it, hoping the fire would take care of itself. Similarly, if you were to feel a lump in your throat or breast, you probably wouldn't just assume it was benign and never get it checked out. That, however, is more or less what most of us do when we feel anxious. We do many things to avoid or run from our anxiety, instead of trying to check it out and see what it's telling us about our lives. We numb ourselves or cause harm to ourselves, without investigating the real source of our suffering.

There's something about the feeling of anxiety that makes people believe it's the problem. I can only assume this is because it's so damn uncomfortable to be anxious. We treat anxiety like it's something unnatural that must be eradicated. Some doctors, psychologists, psychiatrists, and pharmaceutical companies actively push drugs that will reduce our anxiety, which only serves to reinforce this belief. In reality, though, relying on pharmaceuticals has us miss some important clues about behaviors we can be addressing and modifying. I understand that some people really suffer from debilitating anxiety, and medication is a way for them to function in their daily lives. That's fine, too; however, if you choose to take medication, still try to simultaneously work on yourself and address the relationships that are contributing to your anxiety. Also, be aware that numerous studies have demonstrated that people who don't need medication are commonly prescribed it. People who could learn to better manage their anxiety in other ways are taking Xanax and other anti-anxiety medications, which could result in dependency and other issues. *If you really want to get rid of chronic anxiety, you must get clear about how to manage yourself in stressful situations.* Once you do this, the symptoms of your anxiety will actually start to decrease.

Jack came to see me after his anxiety started affecting his work, his functioning, and his personal relationships. He went as far as to fill a prescription for Xanax because it was the way most of his family members dealt with anxiety. However, he was nervous to take it because of the side effects; he didn't want to suffer from weight gain, lose motivation, or become dependent on medications. Jack was born into a hardworking family that made a comfortable living. His father worked a lot, while his mother stayed home to raise him and his sister. Jack explained that his mother had always been a very loving person, to the point that she did everything for him. Even though he was in his 30s, she would buy his household essentials and check in on him weekly to make sure he had food in his fridge. She was always worrying about him and making sure he was okay. Just before coming to see me, Jack lost his job. Unsure about what to do next, he decided to move back in with his parents until he could find another job. Instead of feeling less anxious because he no longer had to worry about paying bills, Jack felt more anxious than ever, yet he couldn't understand why.

If someone is always taking care of you and worrying about you, it's difficult for you to build a mature self. Like Jack, you might end up losing a sense of agency and competency in your life. When Jack moved in with his parents, he started engaging in compulsive online shopping as a way to manage his anxiety. He funneled all his energy into that behavior, instead of taking the time to develop self-awareness and decide what he wanted to do next. Jack would use his mom's credit card to buy himself out of the uncomfortable experiences that, if he had confronted them, would actually have allowed him to develop clarity and self-con- fidence. Jack was feeling unhappy, incompetent, immature, and irresponsible—especially after his mom saw the credit card bill. Instead of getting mad, she had him agree that they wouldn't tell his dad.

Jack explained, "I have financial stability in my family, but feel useless without a job. It made it worse that my mom didn't hold me accountable for my actions." What Jack realized on his own is that when you don't have to work for what you have, it's hard to see its value. Self-confidence and self-reliance are built over time through our experiences; it's not something that can just be handed to us. If we aren't given the opportunity to manage our own difficulties or problems—because we're too busy buying our way out of it or engaging in avoidance behaviors—we'll never develop confidence in our abilities or ourselves. We'll always be anxious when new and challenging circumstances arise, leading us to repeat old patterns in an effort to get immediate relief.

After some time, Jack decided to embrace his anxiety and work with it instead of avoiding it. As he explained, "We don't grow without reaching outside our comfort zones." Self-confidence works just like the muscles in our bodies; it grows according to the amount of effort we put into building it up. If you avoid situations that challenge you, the muscle of your self-confidence will never develop or grow. The same is true if you're a people-pleaser like I was. When you constantly take over for others, you keep them from becoming capable; you contribute to the atrophying of their self-confidence muscle. The "use it or lose it" principle definitely applies here. Jack was used to always getting what he wanted from his mom. He explained to me that "When it comes to finding a job, I just wanted to get there already, without having to fill out applications and go to interviews." If you don't get comfortable with being uncomfortable and only live for instant gratification, you won't ever reach your goals. Jack was able to sit with his discomfort and start working on finding a career, instead of just another job. He moved out of his parents' house, got married, and bought his first home. Once Jack stopped avoiding his discomfort, he was able to grow from it. This process of building self-confidence doesn't happen overnight, and it certainly isn't instantly gratifying.

However, it does help us to better manage our lives and decrease the anxiety that can sometimes overwhelm us.

How Being More Thoughtful About Your Emotions Helps You Self-Regulate

Ask yourself this question: How many of my decisions are motivated by anxiety, and how many are well thought out? When I first asked myself that question and answered it honestly, I got a big wake up call. I realized that many of the decisions I make in my daily life are driven by anxiety and emotions. We all have a tendency to take action as a way to avoid feeling anxious or to make decisions as a way of reducing our discomfort. But in reality, those decisions can potentially create more discomfort down the road. When we make anxiety-based decisions, we aren't being true to what we really want. We act impulsively, which inevitability leads us to feel even more anxious. It's a paradox if you think about it. We make decisions to reduce our anxiety in the moment, only to find that it actually increases over time.

So, what can we do about it? The first thing is to work on ourselves and realize that it's not about what our anxiety wants, it's about what we want. If you know that your anxiety stems from past experiences and is passed on from generation to generation, you can try to get more objective about it. You do this by realizing that even though anxiety is alerting you of danger and telling you to get moving, there probably aren't any legitimate threats nearby. Sometimes it makes sense to listen to your anxiety about a situation—like if you're driving in bad weather, for example—but most of the time, it's just rubbish from the past or worry about the future.

That's why it's important to add thinking to your emotions in the decision-making process. **Ask yourself:** Is this really something to be anxious about? What's the most useful decision I can make under the circumstances? When you bridge that gap between thinking and feeling, you stop bringing past and future anxieties into the present and start solidifying your sense of self. The challenge then becomes keeping yourself from seeking a quick fix or hoping other people will solve your issues for you. When you access your thinking brain during emotional times, you develop your ability to regulate yourself more effectively when your anxiety is high. When we're emotional, we forget that we can meet, be with, and make it through anything if we put our mind to it. And, if you learn to self-regulate through anxiety, you'll eventually develop confidence in your ability to overcome whatever challenges you face.

Like anything worth working toward, this definitely takes some hard work and struggle. There's no way around it! Trust me, I've seen people try. For example, no matter how many times gambling addicts go to the casino, their happiness is short-lived, especially when they're losing. To overcome the addiction and find peace, they have to make concerted efforts—to go to treatment or support meetings, for example, or just say "no"—and experience discomfort. In order to maintain their recovery when inevitable stressors come about, they have to learn different strategies to manage their anxiety. My grandfather used to say, "With hard work and sacrifice comes great rewards." Self-confidence and courage don't come before accomplishing a difficult task; they're the result of working hard and getting the job done.

We all start out hesitant and a little fearful when approaching a challenging task that's of some consequence to our lives. But in order to get anywhere or achieve anything in life, we have to face our fears. As Nelson Mandela once said, "I learned that courage was not the absence of fear, but the triumph over it. The brave man is not he who does not feel afraid, but he who conquers that fear." When you start trying to change your unhelpful behavior patterns, you're going to experience some fear and doubt; but it will serve you to learn to live with those emotions and manage them so that you can keep moving forward toward your goals.

Becoming a confident person is a process of trial and error through which you make your own decisions based on who you want to be within each situation you face. This allows you to better differentiate. I started to develop confidence when I decided to think for myself and move forward with my decisions. As Cheryl Strayed says in her book, *Brave Enough*, "Nobody's going to do your life for you. Whether you're rich or poor, out of money, or raking it in, the beneficiary of a ridiculous fortune or terrible injustice, you have to do life yourself. You have to do it no matter how unjust or sad your circumstances, no matter how hard it is. Self-pity is a dead-end road; it's up to you to drive down it or find an alternative route." What I learned, and what I want to share with you, is that if you want to become less anxious, you must first become confident in your ability to get through this. To reach the ultimate goal of living a less anxious life, you've got to be willing to act for self and put in the work it takes to live a more fulfilling life. Becoming less anxious means working on tasks that build you up and reflecting on the truth of who you are. Would you rather spend your life avoiding anxiety or living in your truth?

When your actions match your values, you feel more in control of your environment. Feeling this way contributes significantly to an overall sense of wellbeing. When what you do is in line with what you believe, your self-esteem and happiness grow. Even if you start taking more risks to act for self, you'll paradoxically feel less fear and anxiety over time. Having a sense of control in your inner world will make you less likely to experience hopelessness, helplessness, or depression. This, in turn, will make it easier for you to take on challenges. Life is not about what other people can do for you; it's about what you create, what you overcome, and what you aim to accomplish.

Learning to Deal with Your Outer and Inner Critics

One of the biggest factors that keeps us from being true to ourselves and reaching our potential is fear of criticism. Even if you don't struggle with people-pleasing behaviors, you're likely to base at least some of your actions on a desire to gain other people's approval in some way; we all do it. Somewhere along the way, you were led to believe that other people's approval gives you value as a person. Maybe your self-worth, self-esteem, and value are tied into being liked and accepted by others. When this is the case, you believe your emotional health is contingent on the approval of others. This idea allows others' actions to dictate your inner experience, which only generates more anxiety in your life.

When we hand over control of our lives, any criticism of us, our work, or our decisions can be devastating. Many people take criticism very personally—mainly because they can't separate themselves from what they can do to prove their worth. Recognizing the difference between the person you are and the things you do is vital in the process of detaching your sense of worthiness from other people's criticisms. Once you become more differentiated and learn to manage your own emotions, your worth as a person will no longer be negated or degraded based on your perceptions of others' negative opinions of you. When you don't act for yourself, other people have power over how you feel about yourself. Remember, as personal development writer Cynthia Kersey reminds us, "the negative comments of others merely reflect their limitations—not yours." The words people say speak more about them than they do about you. If you can keep that in mind the next time someone tries to criticize your life and your choices, you won't take their words to heart or make them mean anything about who you are as a person. Like Eleanor Roosevelt said: "What you think of me is none of my business."

The worst kind of criticism is the kind you internalize and use against yourself, over and over again. I learned firsthand that the inner critic we all have inside of us can be the cruelest and most unforgiving. The anxiety-driven negative narratives we tell ourselves about who we are prevent us from finding our confidence. They lead us to get stuck in jobs we hate, stay too long in relationships that aren't working, and conduct lives that generally lack meaning.

In my view, the inner critic is an echo from the voices of the meanest critics of our past—the teacher, parent, coach, or grandparent who said we couldn't do it. Their voices follow us as we get older and, over time, develop into our inner critic. As time goes on, that critic's voice becomes so loud that it doesn't allow us to chase our dreams, follow our purpose, or realize our true potential. I'm sure you've tried to get rid of that hateful voice by trying to ignore it or, perhaps, listening to what it has to say. Maybe you allow it to tell you who you are and what you're capable of accomplishing.

If you want to stop letting your inner critic defeat you, you first have to come to terms with its existence, understanding that it doesn't speak the truth about who you are and what you can achieve. Critical voices may have you set unrealistic and impossible standards for yourself. Turn down the volume of your inner critic's voice by becoming aware that those thoughts are not your own; they are created from fear and anxiety. Sign a peace treaty with yourself by making the commitment to do whatever you want to do, regardless of what your inner critic says, and to keep moving forward in pursuit of your goals. With every step forward and every personal accomplishment, the voices will get increasingly quieter, until you don't hear them anymore. I think it's important to prove your inner and outer critics wrong. Show them that their words don't and won't speak the truth about who you are and what you can do.

With this as my ultimate goal, I first set out to work on myself and address my people-pleasing issues. I had to learn how to deal with confrontation and tell people things that might displease them. I had to finally stand up for my beliefs and be guided by my own values and principles. I am now thankful every day for the opportunity that life gave me to grow and change. It provided me with the motivation to challenge myself and work on my issues. I used that experience to change into a more confident and self-reliant person. It taught me that the only way to develop independence is to work through tough situations by managing my anxiety, instead of seeking an easy escape. By doing what makes us anxious, we learn to manage ourselves in uncomfortable situations, developing the strength to more effectively deal with difficulties in the future.

To become who you've always wanted to be and do what you've always wanted to do, you'll need courage. Avoiding what makes you anxious won't help you accomplish your goals in life; rather, freedom to have your own life happens when you embrace fear and go for what you want, even when you're scared. After all, bravery and courage come from feeling afraid, yet taking action anyway. So, ask yourself these tough questions: What would I do if I weren't anxious? How would I act if I knew I had nothing to lose? Then take action, and enjoy what it feels like to truly be free.

───────────── SUMMARY ─────────────

Life is meant to be challenging. If you attempt to run away from discomfort, you just end up cheating yourself and guaranteeing that you'll eventually fall even harder down the road. The good news is that in order to be happy and fulfilled, you just need to have your own back and be confident in your skills and abilities. As you become more self-reliant, you'll know that when a challenge arises—and, of course, it eventually will—you'll have all the necessary equipment to get through it. That equipment takes time to gather, and as anyone who lives in Florida knows, you can't scramble to the store on the day of the storm and expect to get everything you need to be prepared.

People aren't born with self-reliance; we gain it through a process of trial and error, as we make decisions throughout our lives in the face of difficulties. People who act with self-reliance feel more in control of their environment, which improves their overall sense of wellbeing. When what you do is in line with what you believe, your self-esteem and happiness grow. You can experience life the way you want to, with less fear and anxiety, while taking more risks and feeling more empowered. Because being self-reliant means doing things for yourself. The more you do for yourself, the better you feel; the better you feel, the more confident you'll become.

ACTIVITY:
DEVELOPING SELF-RELIANCE

For this activity, I'd like you to do something that makes you anxious. Maybe it's talking to your boss about a raise, asking out that person you haven't had the confidence to ask out, interviewing for that job you want, or confronting someone who upset you. This week, try to do that thing you've been too afraid to do. Then, apply that to school, end that relationship, finish that book, say no—whatever it is, do it! And work on managing yourself through your anxious feelings. Use whatever courage you have to speak your mind or act for self. As I've been saying throughout this book, you don't get rid of anxiety about a situation by running away from it; you do it by placing yourself in situations that provoke it. So, now's the time to start doing what you've been wanting to do, especially if it makes you anxious.

CHAPTER 8

COMMON EXPRESSIONS OF ANXIETY

The more we avoid or resist anxiety's presence in our lives, the more control it has over us

FOR MANY REASONS, being chronically anxious is absolutely no fun. But it's the way anxiety tends to express itself in our lives that makes it particularly terrible. Because of it, we might experience panic attacks, negative thinking, constant worry, a wandering mind, the what-ifs, catastrophic thinking, agitation, restlessness, fatigue, irritability, poor concentration, tense muscles, trouble sleeping, avoidance of social situations, and the list goes on. Anxiety plays an instrumental role in determining how joyful and present we are in our lives.

Many of us are embarrassed and ashamed of our own anxious thoughts and actions. We think anxiety makes us weak, and we worry that other people would think less of us if they knew how anxious we actually were. If we allow anxiety to have its way with us, we can wind up feeling shame for the rest of our lives. If we do nothing, we merely carry on the anxious legacy we were born into, automatically repeating the same anxious patterns over and over again. And actually, that's okay. Some people still live a pretty good life repeating patterns and doing what they've always done. But it's more beneficial to your life to carefully examine those patterns, and find out what purpose they're serving. To do this, you can ask yourself questions like:

- Are these patterns useful?
- Has constant negative thinking actually allowed me to function better?
- Has worrying ever helped fix any situation or stopped anything from happening?
- Is catastrophic thinking truthful and honest?

If you asked yourself those questions and answered no to any of them, it could benefit your life a great deal to work on making changes.

One important thing to keep in mind is that telling yourself to stop being anxious may not be enough. You might still think negatively, get overly concerned about the future, or even experience panic attacks. We know that these expressions of anxiety aren't so great, so how do we learn to gain control over them, in order to eliminate them once and for all? When we're anxious, we can feel completely powerless, like we're never going to gain any kind of control over our thoughts, our bodies, or our surroundings. It can feel so uncomfortable to be anxious that we choose to numb ourselves rather than to risk feeling any pain. However, the point of working on ourselves isn't to numb our feelings; we're always going to feel something, and anxiety is always going to try expressing itself in our lives. That's a fact of life. We can try to avoid it all we want, but the more we distance ourselves from this reality, the more control it has over us. *Freedom comes when we can feel anxiety expressing itself, but no longer let it rule our lives.*

Let me be very clear about something again: you aren't weak, and your anxiety isn't your fault. Anxiety is part of everyone's life, and it can strike at any time. Anxiety will still come at times, but we can learn to better deal with it. Most of us think that we should be able to force ourselves to get over whatever is making us anxious. However, when we suffer from anxiety, the goal should never be to force ourselves to feel fine or "normal." It's counter-intuitive, because the more we try to rid ourselves of anxiety and force calmness on ourselves, the worse we get. If you look at the experiences you've had with anxiety, I won't have to do much to convince you of this truth. *The more we try to rid ourselves of worry, negative thoughts, and panic attacks, the more they seem to persist. The more they persist, the more reactive we get to anxiety. And the more reactive we become, the more power anxiety has over our lives.*

When we try to get rid of anything in life, we create resistance; and the more we resist something, the more it shows up. Famous psychologist Carl Jung stated that "what you resist not only persists, but will grow in size." Today, this viewpoint is generally abbreviated to "what you resist, persists," with many kindred paradoxical variants, such as "you always get what you resist." So, the goal here isn't to get rid of anxiety, panic attacks, or persistent thoughts, it's to work on our intolerance of them. It's to learn how to manage ourselves through the discomfort of it all. We don't gain comfort, self-compassion, and calm, by resisting or wishing things were different; we reach true calm by letting it be okay when we're anxious—and letting it go. The more you fight it, the more it will show up; the more you let it be, the less power it will have over you. Again, this is easier said than done. It's a natural instinct to try banishing anything that feels uncomfortable. However, by continuously practicing deep acceptance for what is, we put ourselves in the best position to change it, or even to achieve freedom from it, so that we can move past it.

Defining Panic Attacks

A panic attack can be described as a sudden onset of intense fear or discomfort that reaches a peak very quickly. Some common signs to recognize are:

- Accelerated heart rate
- Sweating
- Shaking
- Shortness of breath
- Chest pain
- Nausea
- Lightheadedness
- Numbness or tingling sensations
- Fear of losing control or "going crazy"
- Fear of dying

Imagine walking alone in the woods, when suddenly you hear a loud noise and see the bushes moving around you. You turn around and see a bear approaching you. Your anxiety rises to panic, and you slowly start backing away. You feel lightheaded, as your heart starts beating faster and you begin to sweat. But because of your quick reaction, you're able to get away. You don't question or criticize the fact that your body reacted in that way. Having encountered a bear, a potential threat to your survival, you find your physiological reaction to be perfectly reasonable.

It wasn't that long ago that intense anxiety was needed to survive day-to-day-life. We had to be on constant alert. But even though times have changed, that alarm system is still very present within us. We constantly scan our surroundings, and even our thoughts, for threats. In fact, panic attacks can be an instinctive reaction to a real threat, or an internally generated reaction to our own thoughts—often those that start with the what-ifs.

When we're anxious, the human brain doesn't know the difference between reality and fiction. It can't tell the difference between something you're thinking about and something that's actually happening. In other words, your brain wouldn't know the difference between you encountering a real bear or thinking about encountering a bear.

Whether you're anxious about a real or imagined threat, your body goes into fight-or-flight mode, sending more blood to your muscles in preparation for a fight or flight from danger. Your heart rate goes up, and less blood goes to your brain, causing you to feel dizzy. Your mouth gets dry. Your breathing pattern changes. Your body produces many different sensations, just as it did when you encountered that bear in the woods. However, when you saw the bear, you were anxious and afraid of the bear itself; you weren't anxious about the actual sensations your body was experiencing. In our modern world, though, when panic hits us randomly, we worry about our feelings. This is understandable; panic attacks that come out of the blue are terrifying. But the more we worry about the expression of anxiety in our lives, the more powerful that anxiety becomes.

So, imagine you experience a panic attack when you're driving in your car, sitting at your work desk, or taking a walk in the park. At that moment, you'll be worried about your feelings. You'll probably judge your racing thoughts, anxious stomach, rapid heartbeat, lightheadedness, or whatever symptom you may be experiencing. That's when anxiety begins to gain control over your life. Panic attacks may start to make more and more appearances in your life, and, the more you try to avoid them, the more they show up. This is another way that our inner alert system warns us of danger. Your brain remembers those times when you were anxious or experienced panic. Consciously or subconsciously, your brain took note of that experience, categorizing it as either dangerous or life-threatening. The next time you find yourself in a similar situation or environment, your brain will alert you to avoid it, and your body will cooperate by producing panic symptoms. Your brain and body are simply helping you stay on guard by alerting you that the last time you were in this situation, you encountered a threat. That's a pretty helpful system. It's the system that kept our ancestors alive, after all. But when your brain starts alerting you about an upcoming flight, presentation, long drive, wedding, or whatever else, it's much less helpful.

In addition to our basic survival instinct, we carry chronic anxiety from our families of origin and absorb anxiety in our current relationships. As I've been saying throughout this book, we as a society are faced with many pressures and non-life-threatening dangers. Things like reaching deadlines, making money, keeping up with the Kardashians, paying the bills, having a career and a family, raising kids with little help, getting likes on Facebook, and responding to endless text messages, are all stressors that our ancestors didn't have to worry about. And guess what? All of those things push our anxiety into overdrive on a consistent basis, without needing to pose any real threat to our lives. What we should really be asking is why more of us aren't experiencing daily panic attacks. Our society is changing at such a fast pace that we've barely had enough time to adapt as a species. The less flexibility we have to adapt to our circumstances, the more anxious, burned out, and sick we'll be. But the good news is, we *can* learn to adapt and make changes!

Changing Our Responses to Anxiety

We've already established that all of us are anxious to some degree or another. We may not be able to change the fact of our anxiety-proneness, but we can change how we interpret our anxiety, and how we respond to it when it appears. When we're anxious, we tend to "story" things in a more dramatic fashion, which can wind up creating more anxiety in our lives. If we can change the stories we tell ourselves when we're anxious, we can change how anxiety impacts us. We only have the power to change our responses, not outside events or people. This change in response lies in deep acceptance, and this acceptance has a calming effect on our nervous system, which gets naturally activated when we're anxious. This is why your response to anxiety matters so much. For example, someone preparing for a big exam might feel her heart racing a little faster in anticipation; noticing this, she might choose to take a deep breath, accept that she's nervous, and move on with her day. Another person in the same situation might feel her heart rate quicken and wind up in a full-blown panic attack. She might start Googling her symptoms and become convinced that something is wrong with her. Because she responds to her racing heart with fear, she stimulates more anxiety and winds up panicked.

Allow me to give you a more detailed example of how our response to anxiety can either help or hinder us. Martha grew up in a home with parents who tended to overreact to many of life's stressors. As she grew older, she noticed that she would react to life in similar ways. She had a long drive to work every day, and she'd often find herself anxious and frustrated in the car. One day, she was driving to an important meeting and ended up in unexpected traffic due to an accident. She found herself stuck with no detours. Her mind automatically began jumping to upsetting conclusions. "What if I get fired for being late?" "I'm going to miss the entire meeting, and my boss is going to yell at me." "I have the worst luck. Nothing ever goes right in my life." Before she knew it, she was in a full-blown panic attack, sweating like crazy, screaming to herself, and honking her horn.

Was it the traffic jam that pumped Martha up to a full-blown panic attack? Was it her parents' fault that she reacted that way? Or was it her reaction to the traffic that created the panic attack? All of the above interacted in such a way that made it predictable for Martha to react so strongly to the traffic jam. She was simply playing out her learned reaction to stressors. Looking at this situation from a systems perspective, it's clear that Martha's panic attack wasn't caused by one particular thing. Although she can't change the past, and she certainly can't prevent traffic jams, she can undoubtedly learn how to better respond when a stressor occurs. Martha pumped herself up so much that she pushed herself into the fight-or-flight state; she communicated to her body that there was a major threat at hand. As a result, her body went into panic mode, and she felt terrified. She wore herself out before she was able to even make it to work.

So, what if Martha could learn how to respond to life stressors in a different way than what she saw growing up? How might she respond differently to being stuck in traffic on the way to a meeting? She could change the way she thinks and learn to say things to herself like, "Looks like I might not make it to my meeting, which stinks. I might as well try not to stress about it, or conjure up every possible worst-case scenario that'll likely never happen. I'm sure my boss will understand. I'm never late, and these things happen. I'd rather be the person stuck in traffic, than the person who got into an accident. Let me pray that they're okay, take a few deep breaths, and listen to my favorite podcast." What difference do you think that response to being stuck in traffic would make to Martha's level of anxiety? How likely would she be to have a panic attack in that situation? By changing the way she thinks, Martha could learn how to calm herself down instead of talk herself up into a full-blown panic attack. She could arrive to work more relaxed, ready to face her boss and the day ahead.

You can alter how anxious you feel about external stressors

by learning to calm your nervous system instead of alerting it to the presence of a threat. This can be done with the power of your thoughts, and with what you choose to tell yourself. It's a choice that isn't all that easy to make; but with practice, over time, your response to stressors can change completely. Throughout this chapter, I'll give you techniques that you can use to change how you respond to your anxiety. It's up to you to choose what you think will work best for you in those moments. I also encourage you to come up with some of your own ideas about what you think will work in your moments of stress.

Fear of Anxiety and Panic Attacks

If every person experiences anxiety and fear, what's the difference between someone who has panic attacks and someone who doesn't? How is it that some people are diagnosed with an anxiety disorder and others are not? When anxiety gets to an unmanageable level, I find that it's often because we've begun to fear the anxiety itself. *When we have a severe intolerance to anxiety, we fuel the anxiety, allowing it to slowly take over different parts of our lives.* Therefore, it's instrumental to change our focus from trying to avoid or get rid of anxiety, to working on our intolerance to it. As counterintuitive as that may sound, try to let that sink in, and really understand how making changes in your response to anxiety can help you make some real changes in your life. When we understand the broader systems at play, we can understand our anxiety mechanisms instead of being afraid of them. We can get a better grasp of whether something is a false alarm, or whether it's time to fight, flee, or freeze. When we see anxiety for what it is, we can also see that it's not useful to listen to our negative thoughts or be guided by what-if thinking. *If we can learn to more effectively distinguish real danger from false danger, we can more effectively respond to whatever situations we face.*

121

When we're anxious, many of us tend to pour gasoline on the fire instead of water. To access water instead of gasoline when we're anxious, we need to be honest with ourselves about what we're experiencing. We have to acknowledge that we hate being stuck in traffic, that we're fearful of flying, that we're nervous to do a presentation, that we aren't okay with telling people what they don't want to hear; and from that place of acknowledgment and acceptance, we need to try our best to be okay with it. Knowing ourselves deeply, and accepting the anxious parts of ourselves, is a way to throw water, rather than gasoline, on the fire.

For example, Frank noticed that he was starting to get a stress headache and feel short of breath. In the past, those physical sensations led to panic attacks and extreme worry. But this time, he took some deep breaths and recognized that his body was trying to alert him of some sort of threat. So, he asked himself, "What am I stressed and anxious about?" Immediately, he remembered the vet appointment for his beloved senior dog, Max, that was scheduled for later that day. The last time he was at the vet, he had to put his cat of 14 years to sleep after she lost her battle with cancer. By simply paying attention, Frank acknowledged that he was anxious about bringing Max to the vet, especially since he was getting older. He was fearful of also losing Max to cancer. But instead of judging himself or becoming fearful of his symptoms, he accepted that his body was merely responding to stress; and although he was nervous, he assured himself that they were just going in for a routine check-up, and Max would most likely be found cancer-free. Frank initially experienced symptoms of anxiety; however, by knowing himself and what happens when he's anxious, he was able to identify his anxiety for what it was. Instead of judging himself and jumping into negative thinking, he validated his feelings and then talked himself down by focusing on the most plausible scenario. When we're anxious, we can easily be blocked from thinking objectively and seeing the facts. When we realize that everyone is anxious about something, that we're all only human, we can be less ashamed of our feelings.

When we can't accept ourselves or our feelings, we become ashamed of who we are. This has an impact on our self-worth and self-confidence. As anxiety expert Geert Verschaeve says, "Anxiety breeds on the gap between the image we want others to have of us, and who we know we really are." It's useful for us to calmly acknowledge and accept everything that makes us anxious; doing so helps us to avoid becoming ashamed of how we feel. Frank accepted that he cared deeply about his dog and that he was anxious about the thought of losing him. And that made all the difference.

Getting Your Life Back

For many of us, our anxiety seems to get worse as we get older. It can take over large parts of our lives, dictating our decisions and critically impacting our sense of freedom. As we've established, and as I'm sure you know all too well already, anxiety is a very uncomfortable feeling. Most of us naturally tend to avoid doing what makes us feel anxious or stressed out. And that makes sense; that's what our brain is telling us to do, after all. However, what if despite that nagging anxiety, you want to go on vacation to an unknown place? What if you want to go to dinner more often and go back to school to change your career? What if you want to get married and have kids? It might feel more comfortable and less anxiety-provoking in those moments to just avoid it, by doing the least scary thing. It's only natural. But avoidance isn't going to make you less anxious in the future; it's actually a near guarantee that anxiety will keep presenting itself in your life. The more you listen to anxiety, the more it believes it's right. The more it believes it's right, the more it's going to alert you to possible dangers down the road. Avoiding situations that make you anxious is only a temporary solution. By engaging in avoidance, you're acknowledging that those situations are, in fact, dangerous and that your anxiety is legitimate. That isn't a long-term solution.

What if instead of avoiding anxiety or trying to control every aspect of your life, which many of us tend to do when we're anxious, you validated your experience, and then worked on forming a deep belief that everything will work out? This is what can help you manage more effectively through anxiety's storms. Think about it: unless you're in a serious life or death encounter with a direct threat to your survival, when does acting on your anxious feelings really serve you? Are you able to make better decisions when you're calm and clear-minded, or when you're anxious and fearful? Most of the things we fear never happen. Understanding this can have a calming effect. However, I've also found that accepting even the worst-case scenarios, and making the decision to be okay, no matter what, is powerful. It's a truly difficult approach to take, especially when your mind goes to extremely dark places; but if you don't want certain aspects of anxiety to control your life, it's helpful to try accepting whatever might possibly happen, acknowledging that most of the time, things work out and take care of themselves.

For many years, I tried to control every aspect of my life. And that worked out well for me... until I had kids. I'd always lived my life with everything planned out, down to the minute. So, when I became a mom, I had a hard time letting go. Planning had always helped me manage my anxiety in the short term; but when things didn't go according to plan, I would get agitated and even more anxious. In a way, having kids taught me how to release control and go with the flow, even if it brought me to do something I didn't want to do. I had to make a choice: I could either be agitated and anxious all the time, or I could accept things as they came.

Although I'll always prefer for things to go according to plan, working on letting go and releasing control has helped me adjust to life as a mom.

For example, I love my sleep and prefer to get an uninterrupted 8 hours every night. That was never going to happen with kids, especially when they were newborns. Just before falling asleep every night, I would ask myself, "What if the baby wakes up every hour and doesn't go back to sleep? What if I sleep through her cries? What if I'm exhausted all day tomorrow?" With some practice, I learned to acknowledge that those what-if scenarios would suck, but I didn't have to keep thinking about them. Instead, I started to tell myself all the ways that things would work out. Somehow, I would find time to sleep. I could always take turns waking up with my husband or call a babysitter for extra hours. I would never get too tired to function, and there was always coffee! What I discovered, is that my anxiety and fear about not getting enough sleep was always worse than actually losing sleep.

The first time I left the country was my first time flying alone as a teenager. I was already triggered since flying meant giving up total control, and flying alone made me even more nervous. When the plane hit turbulence halfway through the flight, my mind started conjuring up all the possible worst-case scenarios, including the ultimate one: that I would die young. But then I remembered something a friend once said to me: "You can't do anything about it if the plane goes down; so you might as well accept your fate in that moment." I felt a calm I had never felt before. I released my need for control, even in the face of the worst-case scenario. In that moment, I accepted my fate, and anxiety no longer had control over me. I realized then that if I could find a way to accept dying young in a plane crash, I could try to apply that same level of acceptance to other areas of my life.

I'm very clear about how anxiety sucks the fun out of our

lives, so I'm by no means trying to downplay the sensations we experience when we're extremely anxious. However, continuing to worry about the worst-case scenarios only serves to start a cycle that makes everything worse. I didn't want to die young in a plane crash; but how would anxiety have helped me in that moment? There was no place to run, and I'm not a pilot, so all I could do was either freak out or accept whatever was going to happen. The urge to freak out and resist what's happening is natural; but we need to ask ourselves: What's a more useful response?

Most anxiety is amplified by catastrophic thinking, which causes your brain to believe that the worst-case-scenario you're imagining is actually happening. In my case, there was no proof that the plane was going down; all that was actually happening was some turbulence, but my mind totally believed that it was all over. However, instead of freaking out and spiraling into a panic attack, I found acceptance. And that was critical. See, you can't fake acceptance. You have to actually mean it. Otherwise, you're just using false acceptance as another form of avoidance to try to get rid of anxiety. When that happens, you stay fearful of the situation and anxiety stays in control of you. Anxiety researcher Dr. Claire Weekes found that as long as we don't accept what scares us, our nervous system will remain under pressure, and our anxiety will continue to grow. Our anxiety wants to be acknowledged; after all, it's probably saved our lives on some occasion. So, there's really no need to fear it. It's just a feeling, a sensation, and a misguided alarm that sometimes goes off when there's no danger present.

Tackling Negative Thinking

Whatever is creating anxiety in your life—whether it's the chronic anxiety of your family of origin, relationships, work, or fear of the future—exploring it and then working to make internal changes will have a significant impact on how anxious you feel.

That part of the change process can't be ignored. However, as most of you know, it's hard to make changes when you're feeling super anxious all the time. Your thoughts are clouded when you're in an emotional state, and this can create a negative-thinking shit-storm that ramps anxiety up several notches. The way this all happens is that usually, we have an experience that makes us feel anxious, and then our negative thinking about it takes us to another level of drama. Without question, all of us can benefit from tackling our negative thinking. Every one of us has a negative commentator in our head, who somehow seems to know all our triggers and insecurities. It knows how to assume the worst of others and project blame for every possible bad thing that could happen to us.

Of course, nobody actively chooses to think negatively. But as it turns out, the more we try to stop our negative thinking, the more negative our thoughts become. These thoughts are manifestations of our anxiety, and they want to be acknowledged as well. They won't simply stop because we try to stop them. So, instead of trying to control our thinking, we're much better off trying to observe our thoughts without judgment, listening to them without letting them define us. When negative thoughts start to swirl around in our minds, we can benefit greatly from taking a moment to think of the actual facts and see through to the truth of whatever we're thinking about. That's the best way of seeing negative thinking for what it really is: B.S! Negative thinking seems to know why your co-worker Jonathan didn't look so enthusiastic to see you; it knows that you're disgusting because you're 10 pounds over your goal weight; it knows that it's all your husband's fault that you have marital issues; and it knows for sure that your turbulent plane is about to crash. It's easy to fall into the trap of believing that our negative thinking has a crystal ball for seeing the future (which just happens to be filled with tragedy and pain). But really, our negative thoughts are only expressions of what we fear; they aren't truth and they certainly aren't reality.

If you fear your negative thoughts or believe that they speak the truth, it won't be too easy for you to face them. But if you can see them for what they are, untruthful thoughts rooted in anxiety, they won't be able to take over your life. When we feel like we're being attacked every day by our own negative thinking, we become alert and on guard. In fact, studies show that our amygdala—the structure of our brain associated with anxiety—grows in size the more anxious and stressed we are. That probably helps to explain why some people get more anxious and stressed as they get older. Conversely, when you make changes and learn better ways to manage your anxiety, you can reduce the size of your amygdala. So, when your negative commentator steps in, first identify what it is. Hear it out, and then say, "Hello, dramatic voice in my head. You almost got me going there. I appreciate you trying to warn me so that I can anticipate all the possible dangers ahead of me. But that doesn't really speak the truth of what's going on right now. If you still want to hang out in my head, that's okay; but I don't believe you to be true." Our negative thinking comes from the most primitive part of our brain: the amygdala. Listening to it is like listening to a teenager's dramatic perspective on life. When our negative thinking is being overly dramatic, it's helpful to recruit the perspective of our pre-frontal cortex—the more mature and logical part of our brain—to help us self-soothe. Then we're able to talk to our negative thoughts like we would to a raging teen who needs help calming down.

I've given you a lot of information in this book so far; however, a common theme in all the chapters has been the importance of observing yourself. Use the knowledge that you've gained to observe what's happening to you. Then you'll be able to identify why you're feeling the way you are. Observing what you're experiencing gives you the option to be curious and neutral, rather than judgmental and resistant. It helps you call out how you're feeling, so you can then say to yourself, "Oh, this is just anxiety I'm feeling because I just missed a call from my brother, who gets me stressed out. He's always calling to complain about something." Simply knowing *why* you feel a certain way can make a world of difference in how you experience it. It can help relax your emotional intensity.

I see this with my own children all the time. When my 4-year-old daughter is having a fit about something, I ask her to identify how she's feeling. She might say something like, "Mommy, I'm mad because I wanted more candy." I don't try to negate her feelings, make her feel better, or give her more candy. I simply reply, "It's okay to be mad when you don't get something you want." Her initial way of expressing her anxiety was to throw a fit. But once we identified her feelings and why she was throwing a fit, we were able to let it be. My daughter doesn't have many fits, and when she does, they're short-lived. I might not have been so lucky if I would have worked hard to make her stop being upset, by giving her what she wanted, or by getting angry with her for being upset. And the same idea applies to us when we're anxious. In fact, there are a lot of similarities between how we treat ourselves and our negative experiences, and how we treat our children and theirs. What if instead of judging and trying to push away our unwanted thoughts and feelings, we call them out, explain why we feel that way, accept it, and then see what we want to do about it? What if we see our expressions of anxiety as akin to a toddler's temper tantrum? The more we give in to them, the more they persist. The more we try to stop them, the more they rage.

One way of utilizing our emotional intelligence is to call out our emotions and figure out what's bothering us. Our goal should never be to eliminate our emotions altogether. Many of us judge ourselves for feeling a certain type of way, instead of accepting that how we feel is how we feel. Rather than resisting our unwanted emotions, we'll do much better if we explain to ourselves what's going on and why it's happening. This form of self-talk will help us grow our pre-frontal cortex and reduce the size of our amygdala.

Applying Mindfulness

A lot of what I've been describing in this chapter can be understood as a way of applying mindfulness to your life. Mindfulness is a state of active attention to the present moment. This means observing our thoughts and feelings without judging them as good or bad. To live mindfully is to live in the moment, instead of dwelling on the past or thinking too far into the future. Mindfulness is a way to identify and manage our emotions and anxiety. It's frequently used in meditation and therapy. It has many positive benefits, including lowering stress, reducing harmful thinking, and protecting us against depression and anxiety. Used properly, mindfulness allows us to be more aware of our physical and emotional state, without getting sucked into self-criticism and judgment. Our experiences are subjective and influenced by our emotional states. Fears and anxiety about the past and the future can make it difficult to appreciate our lives in the present. The key is learning how to pay attention and observe ourselves.

Mindfulness can take place through meditation sessions or smaller moments throughout the day. To cultivate a state of mindfulness, you can begin by sitting down and taking deep breaths. Focus on each breath and the sensations of the moment, such as sounds, scents, the temperature, and the feeling of air passing in and out of the body. Then, shift your attention to the thoughts and emotions you're experiencing. Allow each thought to exist without judging it or ascribing negativity to it. Sit with those thoughts. The experience may evoke a strong emotional reaction. Exploring that response, instead of judging it, can be an opportunity to address or resolve unresolved issues.

There are many ways to practice mindfulness. Some examples are:

Paying attention. As easy as it may sound, it's difficult to just slow down and notice your surroundings, especially when you have a lot on your mind. Make a conscious effort to experience your surroundings with all of your senses—touch, sound, sight, smell, and taste. For example, when you eat a favorite food, take the time to smell, taste, and truly enjoy it.

Live in the moment. Intentionally be open, accepting and focusing on everything you do in the moment.

Accept yourself. We often don't treat ourselves with the compassion we easily give to others. Practice treating yourself the same way you would a close friend, a child, or a loving pet.

Focus on your breathing. When you have negative thoughts, try to sit down, take a deep breath, and close your eyes. Focus on your breath as it moves in and out of your body.

You can also try more structured mindfulness exercises, like:

Body scan meditation. Lie on your back with your legs extended and arms at your sides, palms facing up. Focus your attention slowly and deliberately on each part of your body, in order, from toe to head or head to toe. Be aware of any sensations, emotions, or thoughts associated with each part of your body.

Sitting meditation. Sit comfortably with your back straight, feet flat on the floor, and hands in your lap. Breathing through your nose, focus on your breath moving in and out of your body. If physical sensations or thoughts interrupt your meditation, note the experience and then return your focus to your breath.

Walking meditation. Find a quiet place, and begin to walk slowly. Focus on the experience of walking, being aware of the sensations of standing and the subtle movements that keep your balance. When you reach the end of your path, turn and continue walking, maintaining awareness of your sensations.

Feeling Safe When Anxious

When we're particularly anxious or in the midst of a panic attack, it's also important to find ways to feel safe. I understand that we live in a sometimes dangerous world, and that there are potential threats in our environment. However, we can still find a way to live in the world with confidence in ourselves. It's our perceptions and mindset that ultimately make the difference between feeling safe and unsafe. Realizing that you are your own safety net can help you feel at home wherever you go. If anything does happen, you know you can handle it.

 SUMMARY

If we aren't fearful, we can start to see that our expressions of anxiety are messengers coming to inform us that there's something we need to work on. The techniques I've given you here are intended to help you get through the storms of anxiety, so you can learn to self-soothe instead of throwing gasoline on your anxious feelings. However, if you don't truly work on yourself, those techniques won't get rid of chronic anxiety. If you don't deal with your unresolved issues, the anxiety storms will keep coming. It's finding a way to observe and accept your anxiety that will allow you to start making some real, meaningful, and lasting changes in your response to it. I encourage you to use some of the techniques I've shared to quiet your mind and dig deeper into what's creating so much anxiety in your life. When you begin to lean into your anxiety, you can observe and address it in a way that reduces it.

ACTIVITY:
CHOOSE A TECHNIQUE

It's normal to have negative thoughts. It's part of our evolution to constantly scan our environment, looking for problems to fix. The problem is not so much that we have negative thoughts. Rather, the issues arise when we believe our thoughts are true. Think about an article in a tabloid about the latest celebrity. Most of us know it's an exaggeration or fabrication. We don't believe that the article is totally true, and we don't change our lives around those articles. The negative thoughts in our mind are just like those tabloid stories. The problem is that we don't step back to gain a more truthful perspective. For this activity, I'd like you to choose one of the techniques I described in this chapter or one from the list below, and practice it consistently for two weeks.

Label your thoughts. Instead of saying, "I'm stupid," say, "I'm having the thought that I'm stupid." Instead of saying, "I'm going to fail this test," say "I'm having the thought that I'm going to fail this test." The difference may seem small; however, it can help you gain the perspective that you are not your thoughts.

Thank your mind. If you're having anxious thoughts such as, "I hope this plane doesn't crash," say, "Thank you, mind, for trying to keep me safe. But there's nothing you really need to do right now. I've got it covered."

Let them float away. This one involves imagery. Imagine placing each negative thought in your mind on a leaf, and watch it float down a stream. When you have another thought, as you will, put it on another leaf and watch it float on by.

Sing your thoughts. Try singing your thoughts to the tune of the alphabet song or Row, Row, Row Your Boat. Your thoughts will certainly sound absurd this way, which is the whole point.

Say them in a funny voice. Try saying your thoughts in a funny voice, maybe imitating a cartoon character.

Name your stories. Often, our thoughts are repetitive and involve the same stories. When a thought like, "You're going to embarrass yourself" comes up say, "Oh, here's my *I'm an embarrassing loser* story," and then just let it go.

Do it anyway. Perhaps the most important tip is to remember that you can have a thought and perform any kind of behavior at the same time. If it's something you care about, it's worth it to let the thoughts simply be. You don't have to do anything about them. Remember, you can function even when you're anxious.

I'll cross that bridge when I get to it. When the what-ifs are bombarding you with tales of future disaster, it's helpful to know that you don't need to solve anything right now. When you recognize that you're worrying about a future event, think to yourself, "I'll cross that bridge when I get to it."

CHAPTER 9

SCIENCE-BACKED WAYS TO TAKING BETTER CARE OF YOURSELF

What one can do to take care of self, that will naturally have you feeling less anxious

I F I HAD TO GUESS, I'd say you probably didn't buy or borrow this book to just gain a better understanding of anxiety. No, you want to overcome anxiety, once and for all. You want it out of your life for good! This might have something to do with the shame that tends to come up around suffering from anxiety. It's the reason why so many people get medication prescriptions before they educate themselves about anxiety or try talk therapy. When we believe that experiencing a certain negative emotion means there's something wrong with us, we're likely to seek the quickest fix possible for whatever we feel is broken inside of us. The fix-it mentality is predominant when it comes to mental health concerns—and it's totally understandable. If something is broken, we should take action to fix it. But the information I've provided in this book deviates from the mainstream way of thinking. That's because Bowen theory offers a new way of thinking about anxiety that's hard to translate across paradigms. Rather than focusing on dysfunction, it looks at the broader context in which symptoms arise. The challenge is that when we're anxious, all we really want is relief. Theory stops mattering to most people when their symptoms get overwhelming. But in reality, symptoms offer important information. So maybe instead of running as fast as we can toward the psychiatrist's office for a quick fix, we can start asking ourselves: What is my anxiety telling me?

Research study after research study has shown that medications don't work the way experts would like. Many medications are prescribed to treat anxiety, including traditional anti-anxiety drugs such as benzodiazepines and recent options like SSRI antidepressants. These drugs have been shown to provide temporary relief in some people; however, they come with some significant side effects and safety concerns.

Contrary to popular belief, none of the medications prescribed for anxiety are an actual cure, and recent research has raised many questions about their long-term effectiveness. While they may cure your feelings of worry, they do not cure the root cause of said worries. According to the American Academy of Family Physicians, benzodiazepines lose their therapeutic anti-anxiety effect after 4 to 6 months of regular use. Also, long-term use has been shown to cause brain damage and early onset Alzheimer's disease. Additionally, a recent analysis found that the effectiveness of SSRIs in treating anxiety has been overstated and, in many cases, is no better than a placebo. Furthermore, the withdrawal symptoms for these medications can be serious and often require hospitalization. It's often difficult to stop taking them, and people who wean off of them risk experiencing rebound anxiety that can be worse than their original anxiety.

Now, I certainly understand that if you've been suffering for a while, you'd like some relief right away, and it's totally logical that you'd turn to medication to get it. If you choose that route, the most important thing you can do is become educated about your medications and their side effects. Here are some important questions to ask your doctor:

- How will this medication help my anxiety?
- What are the common side effects of this medication?
- Are there any foods or beverages I'll need to avoid?
- How will this drug interact with my other prescriptions?
- How long will I have to take the anxiety medication?
- Will withdrawing from the medication be difficult?
- Will my anxiety return when I stop taking the medication?

If you have anxiety that's interfering with your ability to function, medication might be helpful in the short-term of your treatment. But keep in mind that many people use anti-anxiety medication when talk therapy or efforts to take care of themselves and work on their relationships would be more useful (and without the major side effects). Anti-anxiety medications can ease the symptoms of anxiety, but they aren't the only answer. I strongly believe that everyone could benefit from evaluating their options and deciding what's best for them.

Throughout this book, I've offered a system and relational understanding of anxiety. I've also given you activities to practice at home. As I've stated over and over again, there's no substitute for taking a closer look at your family of origin, working on developing a self, and becoming a non-judgmental observer of your life. That's a lifelong process of development and growth. But while you work on yourself and gain a better understanding of your family system, there are additional things you can do to naturally decrease your anxiety, which include taking better care of yourself. In the next section, I share some things that you can start doing for yourself, which may help you on your journey to living a less anxious life. Again, there's no substitute for the things I've been discussing in this book; however, I've found that taking better care of yourself reduces daily anxiety quite effectively.

Please Note: This chapter addresses what you can do to take care of yourself. Although these suggestions can be helpful to that end, they don't address how you can manage yourself in stressful situations. You still need to address your chronic anxiety and find ways to respond to it more effectively. Though these natural remedies aren't magical solutions that will lead you to be anxiety-free, taking care of yourself can set you up for major personal growth; it all depends on whether or not you continue to work on yourself. It helps to utilize these natural ways to take care of yourself so that you can face your challenges with a happier and healthier body and mind.

Ways to Naturally Take Care of Yourself

Exercise regularly

Physical exercise has been proven to be good for your physical and mental health. Researchers have found that regular aerobic exercise decreases tension, elevates and stabilize mood, improves sleep, and boosts self-esteem. The findings of several studies show that all you need is about five minutes of aerobic exercise a day to begin stimulating its anti-anxiety effects.

Studies have also shown that exercise is highly effective at reducing fatigue, improving alertness and concentration, and enhancing overall cognitive function. This can be helpful when anxiety has depleted your energy or ability to concentrate. When anxiety affects the brain, the rest of the body feels the impact as well; and when your body feels better, so does your mind. Physical activity produces endorphins, chemicals in the brain that act as natural painkillers and reduce anxious feelings. More specifically, a wide range of yoga practices can reduce the impact of exaggerated stress responses and may be helpful for both anxiety and depression. In this way, studies show that yoga functions like other self-soothing techniques, such as meditation.

Don't drink alcohol

Most of us know that alcohol is a natural sedative, and many of us drink to relax and release tension. However, once the effects of alcohol are gone, anxiety may return with more intensity. If you rely exclusively on alcohol when you're anxious, instead of dealing with what's really going on, you put yourself at risk of developing a dependence. Alcohol is a toxin that can actually induce the symptoms of anxiety. When consumed excessively, it leads to improper mental and physical functioning, negatively impacting the levels of serotonin in the brain.

Stop smoking

Smokers often reach for a cigarette during more anxious times. However, just like alcohol, tobacco offers a quick fix that may worsen anxiety over time. Research shows that the earlier you start smoking in life, the higher your risk of being diagnosed with an anxiety disorder later in life. Research also suggests that nicotine and other chemicals in cigarette smoke alter pathways in the brain that are linked to anxiety.

Say goodbye to caffeine

If you have chronic anxiety, caffeine will compromise your ability to feel less anxious. Caffeine can stimulate nervousness, which is troubling for someone who is already anxious to begin with. Research has shown that caffeine may worsen anxiety by generating an increase in panic attacks among people diagnosed with panic disorder. For some people, eliminating caffeine altogether may significantly improve anxiety symptoms. I'll say a few more things about eliminating caffeine in just a bit.

Get more sleep

Insomnia is a common symptom of anxiety; and, perhaps unsurprisingly, lacking sleep can make your anxiety feel more intense. This is because sleep deprivation creates an imbalance in hormone levels which drives anxiety levels higher. Too little sleep also boosts adrenaline levels which can exacerbate existing anxiety issues.

Try to make sleep a priority by:

- only sleeping at night
- not watching television in bed
- not using your phone, tablet, or computer in bed
- not tossing and turning, but instead getting up and going to another room until you feel sleepy
- avoiding caffeine, large meals, and nicotine before bedtime
- keeping your room dark and cool
- writing down your worries before going to bed
- creating a bedtime routine
- going to sleep at the same time every night

Meditate

One of the goals of meditation is to learn to relax chaotic thoughts and create a nonjudgmental sense of calm and mindfulness in the present moment. Meditation is known to relieve stress and anxiety. Research from John Hopkins suggests that just 30 minutes of daily practice may alleviate some anxiety symptoms and act as an antidepressant. When used properly, meditation allows you to slow down and observe the world without judgment. If you practice it when anxious, it can also help to reduce worrying thoughts and bring about a feeling of balance, calm, and focus. An amazing app that many of my clients use to help them meditate is called Calm.

Eat a healthy diet

Low blood sugar levels, dehydration, or exposure to chemicals in processed foods—such as artificial flavorings, artificial colorings, and preservatives—may create mood changes in some people. Pay attention if your anxiety worsens after eating; if that's the case, it's important to check your eating habits. If you notice that what you're eating is affecting how you feel, try to stay hydrated, eliminate processed foods, and eat a healthy diet rich in complex carbohydrates, fruits, vegetables, and lean proteins. Later in this chapter, I'll share more details on what to eat and what not to eat when you're anxious.

Practice deep breathing

Shallow, fast breathing is common when you're anxious. But breathing this way when your anxiety is high may lead to an increased heart rate, dizziness, lightheadedness, or even a panic attack. Deep breathing exercises—such as deliberately taking slow, even, deep breaths—can help restore normal breathing patterns and reduce anxiety. If you're feeling particularly anxious, deep abdominal breathing can help you relax. Start by inhaling slowly and deeply through your nose. Keep your shoulders relaxed, then exhale slowly through your mouth. As you blow air out, purse your lips slightly, but keep your jaw relaxed. During each inhale, say to yourself, "I know I am breathing in;" during each exhale, say to yourself, "I know I am breathing out." Continue that process until you feel relaxed.

Drink chamomile tea

Chamomile tea is a common remedy for relieving tension and promoting sleep. One study found that people who took a 220-milligram German chamomile capsule up to five times per day showed bigger reductions in anxiety symptoms than people who were given a placebo capsule.

Try aromatherapy

Aromatherapy uses fragrant essential oils to enhance wellbeing. The oils may be inhaled or put in a warm bath or diffuser. Studies have shown that aromatherapy helps induce relaxation, regulate sleep, improve mood, and reduce heart rate and blood pressure.

Some essential oils used to relieve anxiety are:

Lavender Oil

The scent of lavender, the most common essential oil, helps ease anxiety and stress—so much so, that researchers have used it on patients in intensive care units. Several studies have shown that it can be particularly beneficial for people who are sleep deprived.

Rose Oil

Breathing in the scent of rose oil helps promote calmness and reduce tension. It's commonly recommended for people who are grieving a loss or who are feeling depressed.

Vetiver Oil

Mostly popular in India and Sri Lanka, vetiver essential oil is thought of as the *oil of tranquility.* It alleviates emotional stress, anxiety, and depression, and can even help with panic attacks.

Ylang Ylang Oil

Ylang ylang is a tropical scent that's both calming and uplifting. It's known to be the most useful essential oil for boosting emotional wellbeing. It can reduce your blood pressure and has mild sedative qualities, too.

Frankincense Oil

Frankincense oil can lift your mood, boost the oxygen supply to your brain, and stimulate the limbic system, helping you manage your emotions. Many people add this oil to their bath to relax their body and mind.

Geranium Oil

Geranium oil can help you replace negative thoughts with positive ones. Many people believe that it can also help restore hormone imbalances.

Jasmine Oil

Jasmine essential oil has been used for centuries to help reduce anxiety symptoms. Studies have shown that jasmine can stimulate your brain to improve your mood and energy levels. It can also calm your nervous system.

Chamomile Oil

Try inhaling chamomile oil when you're feeling highly anxious or have a tension headache.

Vitamins that help reduce anxiety symptoms:

Magnesium

Magnesium is a natural muscle relaxer, which has been shown to help reduce anxiety. It's a nervous system relaxant and mineral that assists with calming fear, irritability, and restlessness. We tend to store a lot of tension in our muscles, and magnesium offers a natural, easy, healthy way to create a sense of calmness, stabilize mood, and promote a sense of wellbeing.

Passionflower

This is a calming herb used to treat anxiety, insomnia, and even seizures. By increasing levels of GABA [gamma-aminobutyric acid] in the brain, passionflower lets the nervous system relax through the reduction of brain activity, resulting in a decrease of anxiety and stress. For people dealing with insomnia, this herb is extremely beneficial. You can incorporate it into your diet through teas, tinctures, extracts, or tablets. This flower was traditionally used in Europe and the United States to calm hysteria and treat mood dysregulations. **Today, it's most commonly**

used to manage anxiety and insomnia-related symptoms. The more GABA there is in your system, the more relaxed you feel. However, passionflower is not recommended for people taking Paxil or medications with a similar chemical compound. When using it in liquid form, dissolve 3 drops in half a cup of water. It's not recommended to take it straight from the dropper, due to reports that it could cause hallucinations.

Valerian Root

Valerian root has special chemical components that are useful in the treatment of anxiety. Studies have found that specific acids, which turn into GABAs—known, simply enough, as valeric acids—are responsible for inhibiting and regulating the activity of the brain's neurons.

Theanine

Theanine is an amino acid found in green tea, among other places, which causes the relaxed feeling most people get when they drink a cup of tea. Theanine has been shown to reduce stress responses in your body, so that you feel more relaxed, even in stressful situations.

Lactium

When you were a child, your mother likely gave you a warm glass of milk to help you fall asleep. There's a reason for this, and the reason is Lactium, a compound often found in milk. Lactium has been shown to promote feelings of calm and relieve anxiety-related sleep issues.

B-Complex

You've probably heard before that a shot of B12 can boost your mood and energy levels; B-complex vitamins do the same. These vitamins include thiamine (vitamin B1), riboflavin (vitamin B2), niacin (vitamin B3), pantothenic acid (vitamin B5), pyridoxine (vitamin B6), biotin, folic acid, and the cobalamins (vitamin B12), all of which play a role in keeping your mood stable.

Licorice Root

If stress has you feeling exhausted, this one could be for you. That's because licorice root regulates your adrenal glands, which are the stress glands in your body. You see, the adrenal glands release two hormones: adrenaline and cortisol. Those are the hormones that make you feel stressed. But licorice root can help slow the production of those hormones, even fighting adrenal fatigue so you can sleep better at night.

St. John's Wort

St. John's wort is an age-old home remedy for anxiety and mood disorders. It lifts a low mood, decreases anxiety, and promotes feelings of optimism and contentment. Just be aware that St. John's wort may not react well with some prescription antidepressants, so speak to a doctor if you're considering adding it to your regimen.

Ashwagandha

Ashwagandha is an age-old Ayurvedic ingredient that's one of the key components of a mood-boosting supplement. It's considered to be an adaptogen, a natural substance that helps balance the body's reactions to stress. Ashwagandha boosts your mood and promotes restful sleep and relaxation.

Melatonin

Your body creates melatonin on its own, but some people just don't make enough, which can lead to issues with sleep and relaxation, as well as general anxiety. Luckily, melatonin products are available over the counter and can help supplement your body's natural production and regulate your circadian rhythms.

Rhodiola

Known as the *golden root*, Rhodiola has a rich history of medical use in both Siberian culture and traditional Chinese medicine. Rhodiola supports emotional wellbeing and enhances energy levels by helping the body adapt to stress in a healthy way. Rhodi-ola can also support mental energy and focus.

Fish Oil

It's no secret that certain fats are better for you than others, and fish oil is one of them. In addition to supporting heart health, fish oil contains a specific omega-3 fatty acid called eicosapentaenoic acid, which has been linked to mood. Omega-3s are the basic building blocks of the brain and nervous system, so taking fish oil helps maintain a healthy level of cognitive function.

Probiotics

While probiotics are commonly known to support digestion and immune system health, most people don't know that they also have many brain health benefits. Extensive research has found that maintaining an optimal level of gut bacteria promotes a healthy response to chronic stress and has been shown to improve mental health and cognitive function.

Keep in mind that before trying new supplements or making dietary adjustments, you should always speak with your doctor or mental health provider. It's up to you and your doctor to choose the supplement, or combination of supplements, that will work best for you.

Healthy Foods to Reduce Anxiety

There's a growing body of research that suggests that pathways in your gut may affect mental health and anxiety symptoms. This makes sense, given that your gut serves as a protector for the rest of your immune and neurological systems. Taking care of your GI tract through your diet can benefit you in the long-run, offering another way to help regulate your mood.

Veggies, fruits, 100% whole grains, nuts, seeds, and unsweetened dairy products benefit us in numerous ways at the biochemical level. While there's no magic food that can cure anxiety and depression once and for all, there are a few changes we can make to our daily food choices that have been associated with mood-boosting results. If you want to incorporate foods that are tasty, nutritious, and safe, try more of these:

Fermented Foods

Fermented foods like miso, tempeh, sauerkraut, and kimchi contain probiotics, the friendly bacteria that live in your GI tract and help defend against harmful pathogens and microbes. Eating more probiotics can help take care of your gut microbiome, potentially benefiting the gut-brain connection.

Cherries

Cherries contain antioxidants like quercetin, which can help promote feelings of calmness. Eating more fruits and veggies, in general, has also been linked to decreased symptoms of anxiety and depression. Some studies have shown that eating five or more servings per day helps to boost mood. However, according to the Centers for Disease Control, only 10% of Americans meet that recommendation.

Kiwi

Kiwi is full of nutrients like vitamin C, vitamin K, vitamin E, folate, and potassium. Some studies show that the combination of vitamins C, E, and folate may help reduce oxidative stress, which leads to chronic inflammation. They can also promote the production of serotonin, the neurotransmitter associated with wellbeing and happiness.

Seafood

There's evidence to support that an intake of about 8-12 ounces of fish or seafood per week helps boost cognitive functioning and mood, due to the essential omega-3 fatty acids they contain. Try adding more salmon, mackerel, sardines, and shellfish—or algal oil, if you're vegan or vegetarian—to your plate.

Avocado

This nutrient-packed fruit is filled with vitamin B6 and magnesium, a combination that could help with serotonin production in your brain. Adding avocado slices to omelets, salads, and even smoothies, will also help you add more fiber and healthy fats to your diet.

Beans and Legumes

Chickpeas, lentils, beans, and legumes also provide antioxidants, vitamin B6, and magnesium. They're protein-rich powerhouses, so try them as a swap for red meat in your next sauté or stir fry.

Plain Greek Yogurt

Yogurt provides key minerals that may help with symptoms of stress and to stabilize mood; it's also a good source of probiotics. Look for plain, unsweetened versions with at least five strains of live and active cultures to incorporate in your breakfasts and snacks.

Whole Grains

Prebiotics fuel your body's probiotics so they can survive and thrive. You can find them in 100% whole grains like oats, barley, and bran, as well as in various fruits, vegetables, and beans. Eating more of these foods, which have been shown to help reduce the risk of chronic disease, also helps serotonin receptors in your GI tract function properly.

Milk

A cup of milk provides minerals like calcium, potassium, and magnesium. Magnesium, in particular, has been studied for its role in anxiety, yet 68% of Americans aren't getting enough of this important mineral.

Pumpkin Seeds

An ounce of pumpkin seeds provides nearly 20% of your daily value of magnesium, as well as a healthy dose of potassium. Sprinkle these seeds (along with nuts like walnuts, peanuts, pistachios, and cashews) on your meals, or snack on them for a nutrient boost.

Foods to Stay Away From

If you eat lots of processed meat, fried food, refined cereals, candy, pastries, and high-fat dairy products, you're more likely to be anxious.

Caffeine

A known stimulant and psychoactive drug, caffeine has long had a reputation for triggering the body's fight-or-flight response. Caffeine produces sensations that are similar to those of anxiety, such as nervousness, nausea, lightheadedness, and the jitters. If you're suffering from high anxiety, I recommend reconsidering that morning cup of coffee and opting instead for an herbal tea or green juice.

Artificial and Refined Sugars

This one is hard to avoid, because sugar hides in everything! Studies have shown that although sugar doesn't directly cause anxiety, it does create changes in your body that can exacerbate anxiety symptoms and impair the body's ability to effectively cope with stress. A sugar crash is similar to a caffeine crash and can also cause mood changes, heart palpitations, difficulty concentrating, and fatigue— all of which can be interpreted as the beginning stages of an anxiety or panic attack.

Gluten

Gluten is a protein found in wheat, barley, and rye products. For many anxiety sufferers, gluten can also be a huge trigger for anxiety symptoms. Research has now confirmed that people with

Celiac disease and gluten intolerances are at higher risk for anxiety, depression, and other mood disorders. Talk to your doctor about getting tested for Celiac disease or gluten intolerance. Cutting gluten out of your diet could be the difference between living with anxiety and managing it for the better.

Processed Foods

Generally, processed foods are high in the previous two items mentioned on this list, as well as a bunch of additional additives and preservatives. Refined flours and sugars are said to feed the harmful bacteria and microbes in the gut. With more research being conducted, the general consensus is that gut health is a major contributor to chronic anxiety, and many mood disorders can be treated by proliferating good bacteria in your gut.

Dairy

About 10% of adults are lactose intolerant, and even more are thought to have difficulty digesting the casein found in cow's milk. Dairy is inflammatory. It can wreak havoc on the digestive system, causing, bloating, diarrhea, and constipation, among other things. If you're sensitive to dairy, it might be creating more anxiety in your life.

Soda

In addition to the artificial food coloring and additives found in soda, aspartame is one of the most common ingredients found in things like diet soda and chewing gum. In addition to blocking the production of serotonin in our brains (like sugar), Aspartame is also believed to be responsible for headaches, insomnia, anxiety, and mood swings, and has been linked to certain forms of cancer.

Fried Foods

Not only are fried foods difficult to digest, they also have very little nutritional value. Combining poor food choices with unhealthy cooking processes is a sure way to exacerbate your anxiety symptoms. Most fried foods like French fries, fried chicken, and onion rings are cooked in hydrogenated oil, which not only contributes to weight gain but is also horrible for your heart. Fried foods increase your risk of high blood pressure and heart disease.

Fruit Juice

Fruit juice, just like soda and other store-bought beverages, is packed with sugar. There are three different types of sugar: sucrose, glucose, and fructose. Fructose is the sugar naturally found in fruits and vegetables, which is usually added to fruit juice and fruit-flavored drinks. The problem is that the body only processes fructose in the liver, which is not the body's preferred energy source. What protects us from absorbing too much fructose when we eat fruits and vegetables is the natural fiber in those foods. When we get rid of that fiber, we put our bodies at risk of overconsumption. So, if you want fruit juice, make it at home. I recommend sticking to the 80/20 rule, making juices that are high in leafy greens and lower in fruits.

Foods High in Sodium

Researchers have concluded that too much sodium in our diets can have a negative effect on our neurological system, causing fatigue and damaging the immune system. Salt is essential to maintaining good health and a balanced diet, but too much can increase anxiety, panic, and depression. Not to mention, the overconsumption of sodium leads to weight gain, high blood pressure, and water retention.

SUMMARY

This chapter provided you with lots of information on natural ways to take care of yourself. This might be reassuring for you, or it might be overwhelming. Just keep in mind that these aren't cures of anxiety, but rather suggestions to help you on your path to living a less anxious life.

There are so many resources and options out there, I know it can be hard to choose. But just start small. Add a vitamin you feel comfortable taking, or make an effort to unwind with a cup of chamomile tea instead of wine before bed. Personally, I've found a system that works best for me, which doesn't include everything I listed in this chapter. I take magnesium, fish oil, and vitamin B in addition to my multivitamin. I drink chamomile tea after dinner, meditate for 10 minutes before bed, maintain a healthy diet as part of my lifestyle, and exercise 5 days per week. Once a month, I treat myself to a 90-minute lavender oil massage. I try to get at least 8 hours of uninterrupted sleep a night, depending on my kids, of course. I've also continued to work on myself and my family relationships by going to therapy when I feel overly stressed, and attending a Bowen group training once a month. All of this has contributed to many positive changes in my life, including a significant decrease in my anxiety. I used to experience weekly panic attacks, regular migraines, frequent pinched nerves, and severe pain in my neck and shoulders. Before I changed my diet, I had heartburn almost daily, which usually caused me to stress out even more. Today I can tell you that I haven't had a panic attack in over 10 years. I might get a migraine twice a year, but I haven't had a pinched nerve in over 8 years, my neck and shoulder pain doesn't bother me nearly as much as it used to, and I very rarely get heartburn. I'm telling you this because even though getting rid of anxiety isn't as easy as taking a pill, there are natural remedies out there that will work for you; you just have to be motivated and determined enough to make changes in your life. It won't happen overnight, but I'm not sure what could be more important than working toward a happy and less anxious life, filled with joy and positive relationships.

ACTIVITY:
CHOOSE A NATURAL REMEDY

For this activity, choose one natural remedy to try (maybe exercise, yoga, supplement, or meditation), one food to add to your diet, and one food to eliminate. Try this for one week and see how anxious you feel. Notice if these changes help you manage your anxiety more effectively, especially when you're around your opinionated father, negative spouse, hyperactive child, or demanding boss. If you like the way you feel, keep going with the changes you made. Then, try something new every week, until you find the right system that works for you.

Footnote: *citations for the research I mention in this chapter can be found in the bibliography at the end of the book.*

CHAPTER 10

WORKING ON DEVELOPING A MATURE SELF

Developing a mature self is a lifelong process,
not an endpoint

WHEN I WAS ANXIOUS, experiencing regular panic attacks and dealing with anxiety-related health issues, I had no idea what was happening inside of me. For me, the "not knowing" was the scariest part. I went down many roads to find answers, but nothing stuck or made much of a difference in my life—at least not for the long term, anyway. When I finally did find answers that made sense to me, it's like all the stars aligned and my life experiences finally had some meaning. But I never could have figured it out on my own. That's why, after changing my own life, I decided to become a writer. I wanted to go beyond the therapy setting and share what I learned with others. I wanted to reach more people. Never in a million years would I have guessed that the one thing missing in my life—the thing that could change everything else—was, in fact, me. It seemed like I was a *self*. I had a name, an identity. I held a driver's license and a social security number. But those things weren't proof that I was a solid and mature self. They were only proof that I was born.

You see, I used to be a damn good chameleon. I was amazing

at blending into the background, always careful not to create any waves. I merely existed, in the simplest sense of the word. I didn't have any values, goals, or principles of my own. My thinking mostly came about from the force of togetherness. I forged my identity by taking on others' opinions as my own, responding in ways to appease the people in my life, and only feeling happy when everyone else was happy. When the people around me were in pain, I was in pain, too.

That's what I see with a lot of my clients and people I encounter. It's like their brains and emotions are highly intertwined with others, attached by an invisible electrical wire. If only we could find a way to be ourselves, feel how we want to feel, and respond how we want to respond, despite being so interconnected with others. If someone I love hurts, it doesn't feel good to see them in pain. But I've learned that while I can deeply acknowledge what they're feeling, their pain is not mine. To me, being a self isn't about totally disconnecting from others, because we can't do that anyway. It's about knowing how interconnected we are and accepting our human condition, but still trying to be our own separate person. If you're having a bad day, it doesn't mean I need to have a bad day, too. If you're a die-hard Republican, it doesn't mean I need to share your views.

The beauty of *Family Systems Theory* is that it sees individuals in their context and appreciates the major dilemma we all face when attempting to be our own person. A big absence in clinical psychology theories is the acknowledgment that being human is a relational experience. We can't understand individuals without looking at them in the context of their families. The main message of this book is that you can't understand what's happening with you until you understand your relationships. The only way to develop a mature self is within those very relationships. Every one of our relationships plays a key role in increasing our self-awareness and helping us become a mature self.

The very relationships that created stress and anxiety in my life were the ones that helped me the most on my personal growth journey. You see, nothing outside of me had to change for me to be less anxious; I had to create real change from *within* myself while staying connected to the ones I loved. Long-lasting change takes place when we can look in the mirror and ask ourselves: How am I contributing to the problems I'm currently facing? What can I do to define myself in this relationship?

There are many ways that we can learn to better manage our anxiety and get to a better place in our life. However, I've found that maturing and developing a self creates a powerful shift that brings about long-lasting change. *The more solid our sense of self becomes, the less spooked we are by the things that made us anxious in the past.* We grow in our ability to observe our environment and become more factual than emotional in our responses. In the work I've been discussing throughout this book about becoming more differentiated—more of a *self*—motivation and determination go a long way. This motivation and determination can allow you to do the work that bridges the gap between your emotions and intellect. My hope is that this book will give you the tools to integrate your thinking and emotions when a difficult situation presents itself—a sturdy bridge that won't crumble, even in the worst of storms.

When we're anxious, we can get curious about a few things: How can I focus on myself? How can I be more thoughtful, instead of reactive? How can I manage myself through this, while still sticking to my values and principles? How can I find a way to manage myself, rather than projecting my anxiety onto others? The steps we take toward becoming a mature *self* are never perfect. When I first started out on this journey, I wasn't the most elegant in my attempts to define myself in my relationships. It takes a lot of trial and error as any new behaviors do. And it helps to accept that there's no such thing as quick fixes, especially when it comes to our anxiety. A major challenge to being more of a mature self is having the ability to tolerate how slowly real change takes place. It's also tough to make changes when you receive pushback from people in your life who don't agree with you being more of a mature self. As Jenny Brown, MSW beautifully says in her book *Growing Yourself Up:*

> "This process of being mature…has been likened to learning to sail against the wind; and as any sailor will tell you, this requires concentration and tolerating some tension as the wind pressures the vessel to let it take over the controls. Good skippers know how to tolerate sufficient tension to keep a steady course. They don't try to overpower their vessel with too much sail in order to get to the finish line faster, as they know this will inevitably knock them backward. They also know not to panic and retreat to the safe harbor of familiarity. They focus on their key tasks of setting the course and letting the crew know their intentions so that each person can get on with focusing on their own tasks. There's only one path to growing this ability: through patience, thoughtful perseverance in the midst of experience…no shortcuts to be found."

For example, ever since Hailey could remember, she was a sounding board for her mother. Every day, her mother would call her and project her daily grievances onto her. Her mother was very anxious and short-tempered, so there were a lot of things she'd get upset about. Hailey saw herself as easygoing, and couldn't understand why her mother was always upset. After her daily phone call was over, Hailey would feel like a huge weight was clutched around her neck. She would often think to herself, "Why can't my mother just be more positive? Maybe if I was a better listener or advice giver, she could learn to be happier. How can I get her to stop complaining to me without upsetting her? I should stop taking her phone calls, but what if she hurts herself? I'm so selfish for thinking of myself. My mother needs me." What a burden for Hailey to carry! How could she not be anxious when talking to her mother?

Most people would see Hailey's mother as the one with the problem. It's easy to see her as the one who needs to learn how to cope with her anxiety, without projecting it onto her daughter. It's natural to believe that she's the one who needs to change for Hailey's benefit. But what if Hailey learned to *define* herself in those conversations with her mother, instead of thinking that she needed to take on her mother's concerns? What difference do you think it would make if she learned to manage her own anxiety around her mother's discomfort? What if she no longer felt the need to solve her mother's problems? How can she begin to think for herself, be supportive, and not feel like she has to fix anything? Well, for starters, she can do this by being willing to *define* what she's willing to do and become realistic about what she can really offer. Many of us try to calm the person who's upset; however, it's actually more useful to calm yourself down, while in that person's presence. Dealing with our anxiety around others isn't about working hard to change them. It's about looking at our own responses to them and thinking about how we can change our responses so that we speak up for ourselves without taking blame.

If you have a chronically anxious family member whose presence tends to make you feel more anxious, consider how many of your attempts to change them have actually worked. By taking the approach of calming ourselves in the presence of their anxiety, we have the ability to learn and grow, while still being who we are. Hailey learned to continue being a *self* in the presence of her mom's anxiety, by not taking it on as her own, and by bringing up things that were going on in her own life. She also committed to no longer answer the phone when the timing wasn't convenient for her. Hailey explained, "My mother called me very upset the other day. But I managed myself through the call and told her, 'I'm sure you will figure it out.' Then I told her about my day. After we hung up, I didn't feel any weight around my neck, or any need to be in a bad mood afterward. I realized in that moment, now I am free." Hailey found a way to calmly listen to her mother, without letting the *togetherness force* pull her into choosing how to respond. Think about how much of our anxiety can decrease in all areas of our lives, if we learn to apply clear thinking in the presence of others' anxiety. All of us have a logical *self* that can help us resolve life's issues; the challenge is to forego our urge for quick fixes and stop looking for others to give us a magic solution. We need, instead, to ask ourselves, "What can I do to more effectively address these issues? How can I be more of a solid self in the presence of anxious people?" When we don't have a mature *self*, we live at the mercy of our anxiety-producing circumstances. As Michael Kerr said in *Bowen Theory's Secrets*, "People with more of a 'self' have less intense reactions, more accurate perceptions…and more ability to self-regulate the behaviors that those reactions can evoke."

If the concept of a solid self is still unclear, consider the characteristics below. **People with a solid self:**

- Are accepting of their feelings, without allowing them to overtake their decision-making.
- Don't expect to be instantly gratified.
- Work on developing their guiding principles.
- Look at how they can contribute to resolving issues, instead of placing blame.
- Find a way to accept people who don't have the same views as them.

- Try and stay connected with their loved ones.
- Take responsibility for finding solutions to their own problems.
- Allow others to solve their own issues.
- Keep in mind the bigger picture.
- Regulate their own emotions.
- Are more flexible in their daily lives.
- Have lower levels of chronic anxiety.
- Engage in emotional cutoff less often.
- Look at individual behavior in its context.
- Are interested and informed but remain focused on their own lives.

Developing Core Beliefs

There's a lot of value in sensibly contemplating what beliefs and principles guide your life choices and behaviors. Most of us just go along with the beliefs we were born into; we act in ways that fit with our parents and culture, without necessarily questioning if they fit with who we are. Most families have religious and/or cultural traditions that span several generations. And while there's plenty of value in having family traditions and religious faith, we often partake in many of those traditions without asking ourselves if we genuinely want to participate in them. When we choose to follow traditions just because our parents chose them, or when we reject those traditions without knowing much about them, we aren't operating from a solid sense of self. Coming up with our own core beliefs is about more than just automatically accepting or rejecting certain sets of beliefs. It's about taking our time to examine and explore what we believe in. It's about asking ourselves, "What values do I want to live by?" I know it seems a lot easier and more acceptable to just follow along with what your family has done for many generations. And that's totally fine if it's what you truly want to do. But, if you can take some time to reflect on what's truly important to you, you'll be more likely to follow the guiding principles that come from you, rather than the ones you think you "should" follow.

When it comes to our own beliefs about life, morality, and spirituality, it's easy to be driven by anxiety. However, it's useful to find ways to adopt our own beliefs about what we truly think. Personally, I'm a born skeptic. Sometimes I wish I could just blindly accept the traditions I was born into. For a while, that's exactly what I did. I pretended to believe in things I wasn't convinced about and made decisions based on other people's values. But in the end, my natural skepticism won, and I began to figure things out for myself. Born into a Jewish family, I was raised with a certain worldview, a particular set of guiding morals, and a variety of traditions that I participated in without question. Going to a religious school most of my life probably had a different effect on me than my parents would have liked. As much as I tried, I just couldn't connect with the very religious way of life. I did, however, connect with many of the Jewish traditions, because I found it fascinating that I could do things my ancestors once did. It made me feel close to them in some way. My own faith grew when I decided to learn about religion and spirituality on my own. By doing so, I discovered the origins of my morals and my ideas about what it means to be a good person. I found that all religions, at their core, have very similar principles. I decided to continue in my Jewish faith, as a way to be close to my ancestors. It also gave me a way to connect to a G-d that I chose to not only believe in, but have a relationship with as well.

You might be wondering how a book about anxiety, whose origins come from Natural Systems Theory and evolution, suddenly became spiritual. It's because I believe that evaluating

162

our beliefs, which can include our religious beliefs, gives us an opportunity to grow. It helps us develop confidence in what we believe in, how we decide to live our life, and it can give us an inner calm in the face of adversity. It's one way that we can bridge the gap between our emotions and intellect. When we take a more mature look at our religion, values, and beliefs, we can remain thoughtful in our own ideas about life. Religion is where many of our morals, principles, and ideas about life came from. So, it makes sense to look back at them, choose what fits for us, and live accordingly.

I wrote my second book, *It's Within You*, with a Chabad Rabbi. It gave me a way to reconnect with the Jewish values and principles that have always guided my life in some way. In writing that book, I came to realize that my skepticism toward my religion wasn't about its teachings; it was more about the extremist push for the exclusion of people who don't follow what you follow. The Rabbi I worked with accepts everyone he encounters; he finds the worth and value in all people, regardless of how religious they are. I find myself taking the same stance. I think one of the most beautiful things about life is that we all get to interpret it in our own way and decide what makes sense for us. One of my guiding principles is to be accepting of others' beliefs and stay openminded and curious about other people's opinions. As far as we know, no one holds the ultimate answers for the best way to live. No one knows the absolute truth about which values or what religion is the best. So, a critical aspect of developing a mature self is finding your own truth, without trying to impose that truth onto others. Developing your own core beliefs isn't about trying to be consistent with others, or to think the same way as the people around you; it's about having your own unique voice in the mix.

Resolving Unresolved Emotional Issues

I truly believe that we all want a better-functioning self and happier families. And I think most of us try our very best to reach that goal. However, we also aren't very tolerant of the inconveniences and uncomfortable circumstances in life. We're especially uncomfortable with the idea that we have to make changes within ourselves and our behaviors to work toward a better life and family. We're up against a lot when we try to make changes, depending on our current circumstances and family history. I think one of the more difficult tasks is resolving our unresolved emotional issues—the ones we tend to blame on our parents and the previous generation. Instead of blaming the past, we have an opportunity to grow, by considering how our own behaviors are perpetuating the patterns of the past in our present life. It's important to remember that working on ourselves and trying to resolve what's been unresolved doesn't mean placing blame on ourselves. It also doesn't mean excusing people for their bad behaviors. It means taking responsibility for our own lives, here and now, and knowing ourselves so well that we can recognize our anxiety-driven patterns and try to do something more thoughtful instead. It means being who we want to be, no matter how hard it gets when anxiety hits.

Having suppressed emotions or unresolved emotional issues holds us back from making decisions as a solid self. When things from the past have been left unresolved, we're likely to subconsciously repeat patterns, instead of consciously making choices. You might be wondering, "What does this actually mean?" If you've had a traumatic event, negative experience, or difficult relationship with a caretaker in your past, you might be making a lot of your current decisions based on fear and anxiety. In that case, you've become limited in your ability to change certain patterns. Your emotions take over you when you're in an emotionally compromised position. When this happens, you stop maturing. Your life, choices, and reactions become quite repetitive.

If we never resolve emotional pain, wherever it derived from, we're more likely to contribute to the chronic anxiety and lack of self we have now. As a result, we avoid situations that could make us vulnerable to experiencing similar pain again, or we jump into relationships that recreate that pain. Many of us think that resolving issues means waiting for the person who hurt us to acknowledge how they impacted us and apologize for it. However, that doesn't happen most of the time. Many people are either unable or unwilling to take ownership of their actions. They may even continue to do what you find hurtful, showing up as the same person they've always been. We have to resolve things within ourselves, without waiting for others to make things right. I know this all sounds unfair. It's hard enough to resolve issues when we actually do get an apology. However, resolving the past isn't only about the people or events that have harmed us. It's about keeping the pain from repeating itself or making us prisoners to our own circumstances.

Jacob came to see me after cutting off from his father, who would often drink excessively and then criticize Jacob for mistakes he had made in the past. He was tired of hearing what a terrible person he was, even though he knew he wasn't one. Looking back at his family history in our sessions together, Jacob saw that his paternal grandfather was also a regular drinker who would become critical under the influence. He was sure that his grandfather acted the same way toward his dad. Recognizing these similarities helped shed a little light on what must have been going on with his father; however, he assumed that his father's experience with this kind of abuse should have kept him from repeating it with his own son. Further into our conversations, Jacob mentioned that his long-term girlfriend would regularly call him a perfectionist and tell him he was often critical of her. He explained that he didn't even notice the criticism, because it was so automatic for him. He realized that it was probably the same for his father. Jacob saw that if he didn't resolve his feelings of being criticized, he'd probably do the same thing to his future children.

Through the awareness he gained, Jacob came around to working on his relationship with his father. He did it by being more of a *self* in his presence, by not taking his critical comments personally, or regarding them as the truth about who he is. He also made it clear to his father that he wouldn't hang out with him while he was drinking. He began to understand that his father was projecting his unresolved issues onto him, and that he didn't have to internalize those projections. By recognizing the automatic process behind his father's actions, and subsequently setting clear limits with him, Jacob found his way to empathy and forgiveness.

It's important to note that when it comes to healing unresolved emotional issues, you don't have to talk directly to the person who has harmed you and reopen wounds about the past in a confrontational manner. The value of getting a broader picture of the past isn't that it lets you place blame, but that it lets you gain more knowledge and awareness about the patterns before you. This knowledge can help you *move forward in your life* like Jacob was able to do in his life. Jacob felt some fear and anxiety in his father's presence, but he moved forward anyway. He quickly realized that he could be around his father *and* hold on to himself at the same time. He said, "I can handle it." And you can handle it, too. Even if things fall apart or don't work out the first time, you can keep your commitment to resolving relationship issues, no matter what happened in the past. This is how confidence in yourself is developed. But remember, as I've said before, there's no one-size-fits-all strategy for this process. Your safety and well-being always come first. So, as always, work on what feels useful to you, and reach out to a professional or trusted loved one when you need some support.

Crisis, or Opportunity for Growth?

Reflect for a moment on the following questions: What's the first thing you do when you feel uncomfortable? Do you spring into action or avoid doing anything, when the going gets tough? Take a moment to reflect in order to see if those things are working for you? Are you finding the fastest way to safety and comfort, or do you actually work through the issues that arise? Do you throw a fit? Overwork yourself? When things don't go according to plan, most of us regress, leaving ourselves behind. We act on impulse to satisfy our wants, and we lose ourselves whenever something makes us uncomfortable. The real challenge for us under such circumstances is to avoid dwelling on the negative parts of life and instead think about how we can more appropriately deal with life's inevitable disappointments. How you perceive a crisis and decide to act in response to it, can make the difference between effectively growing from the experience, or regressing into old, unhelpful patterns.

When a negative situation arises, instead of disconnecting from it immediately by going into thoughtless action, look within yourself and ask, "What type of person do I want to be in this situation?" Think about how you would like to respond, instead of how your impulse for comfort would prefer that you act. Then do what you think or believe is right. Or, alternatively, do nothing. Sometimes it's okay not to respond. However, always take a moment to acknowledge and appreciate the situation, instead of giving in to the urge to do something about it.

When you're faced with difficult situations in life, try to see them as opportunities for you to decide who you are, and to see what you're capable of. When you continue to act in certain ways just to avoid hurt, you rob yourself of the opportunity to experience who you can be in different situations and circumstances. How you choose to behave, think, and feel are all expressions of who you are. When you observe your self without judgment or impulsivity, you're making a decision about who you are; you're being more of a mature self. Situations in life, especially negative ones, can always serve as opportunities. When you can start to see them that way, you'll no longer need to engage in harmful behaviors to avoid them. Instead, you'll be able to respond to things more mindfully and thoughtfully. You'll be an active participant in your own life. There are a few ways that you can practice being more of a mature self when a crisis arises, allowing yourself to move through setbacks without creating more drama in other aspects of your life:

1. Make a real effort to have your feelings line up with your logical brain by looking at the facts of the situation.

2. Practice sitting with the discomfort that comes from your wants not being immediately satisfied.

3. Think about your personal values instead of imposing them on other people.

4. When people in your family system upset you or you don't agree with them, try to stay connected to them rather than pulling away.

5. Remember that you are not responsible for other people's problems, and they need to find their own way.

6. Have your own ideas, values, and thoughts—even if others disagree with them.

7. Look beyond your initial impulsive reactions, so you can see your real intentions, and act in ways that align with who you want to be rather than what your impulses dictate.

Living with a Purposeful Self

Many of us have heard about the importance of living with purpose. We often associate that with the type of job we have or the work we do. Although that may be part of it, I see living with purpose as being able to express who we are in everything we do. Living with purpose is more about expressing who we are in how we live. We live with purpose when we can be ourselves in whatever circumstances we face, holding on to our values, and making a unique contribution to our families and communities. I've given you a lot to process in this book. There's work to be done if you want to truly live a less anxious life. However, all I've done is to teach you a bit about Natural Systems Theory and shed some light on why you're anxious; what you do with this information is up to you. For me, and the many people who have done this work, going through the personal work of developing your self opens up the door to living more purposely and intentionally. I know it can feel constraining and hopeless to learn that much of your behaviors have been automatic. But as a perpetual optimist, I prefer to see the freedom this theory offers. It frees us up to be who we want to be, even in the face of a difficult family life, trauma, and crippling anxiety. No one wants to suffer; but knowing there's purpose, growth, and meaning to that suffering, makes it a lot easier to manage.

When we live as a more purposeful self, we can ask ourselves: How can I know what I'm clear about and then communicate that to others? What's authentic about me? How can I think about things more objectively? How can I respond to what is, rather than get caught up in what should be? Remember, you're more valuable to yourself and others when you operate as a whole self. More highly differentiated people are able to observe things clearly and set purposeful goals, even when they're stressed or anxious. Less differentiated people, on the other hand, have fewer options for responses and are more susceptible to feeling vulnerable and helpless. Self-regulating and being resourceful, requires the ability to engage with our problems. It takes emotional strength and purpose, to keep defining who we are in the face of high-stress situations. Keeping this perspective in mind can help calm you down.

When you can expand your perspective, you can take charge. When you can see that there's a bigger picture at work, you can start to relax instead of acting as if you've never faced challenges before. You can ask yourself, "How do I think I can handle this challenge?" "What do I think will be useful in this situation?" This process will give you some autonomy in the choices you need to make. The big challenge is to sit through this process and remember that small changes add up over time. It's the accumulation of those small changes that leads to true and lasting freedom.

SUMMARY

We're all born with a script. We can follow that script, or we can make this life our own, by developing our character the way we want it to be. Once we're aware of our process and how our own family system works, we become free to decide who we want to be, and how we want to express ourselves.

One way we *manage stress* is to avoid anything that makes us anxious. Another is to face it, knowing that it will make us uncomfortable. In the short term, we might feel more stressed by taking this approach; but in the long term, we'll wind up feeling a lot more comfortable and confident. There's always going to be stuff in your life that you'd prefer didn't happen. Life is filled with challenges, but you can trust in your ability to figure them out. *Differentiation of self* is a lifesaver. When you're in the waves of emotions, having a *mature self* will help you stay afloat. It will help you take a leap of faith and do things you want to do, by simply looking *within* yourself for the answers.

This book is, admittedly, a bit less cheerful than my previous writings. My intention of writing it was to present the facts of anxiety, in the hopes that you'll find it useful and relatable in some way. At first read, the truths in this book can be a punch in the gut; but over time, they can be freeing. Most of us spend our lives putting bandages over our splinters. But even though it hurts, I think it's more useful to pull out whatever's stuck inside of you and stitch it up properly. At first, it might hurt more than simply covering it up, but it will serve you much better in the long-run. This is an opportunity for you to understand your pain, deal with the real issues, and find authentic ways to engage with what's most important to you. It's time to pull out the splinter and live your life as your truest, most intentional self.

ACTIVITY: WORKING ON DEVELOPING A MATURE SELF

So, what constitutes a mature self? It's the ability to know yourself—to be able to accurately assess your strengths, weaknesses, purpose, and potential. It's also the ability to be honest with yourself and to be true to who you are and what you value. It's the ability to take responsibility for your choices and actions. The ability to accept yourself as you are, knowing that you can improve and develop any aspects of yourself that you choose. Sounds simple enough, right?

If you haven't already caught on, developing a mature self takes deliberate action and concentrated effort. It takes acknowledging your value as a human being, and then working to gain the skills needed to confront the many challenges and adversities you'll encounter in life.

When you possess a *solid and mature self*, there isn't much that can rattle you or break your stride. You're able to be confident, poised, and assured, because you know you're equipped to handle whatever comes your way.

For this activity, think about a situation you're currently facing that's been really challenging for you, then reflect on the following questions. How do you think you've been handling the situation? Would you like to deal with it differently? How can you start to see the situation as an opportunity to develop your mature self? What difference would it make if you were able to respond as a mature self? Write about how the past might predict your response to the situation, and then write about how you're going to deal with it moving forward. Lastly, write about the possible positive effects this new response will have on your anxiety.

FINAL THOUGHTS
ON ANXIETY

W E ALL WANT TO UNDERSTAND why we sometimes feel the way that we do. The unknown doesn't sit too well with us. When it comes to the cause for our feelings, we all want answers, and we want them now! No wonder we invented search engines. What's better than having the answers to our questions at our fingertips? Yet somehow, in spite of all the plausible answers that experts, Google, and our family members offer, we're still anxious. Even exciting changes can heighten our anxiety levels, leaving us feeling stressed out and overwhelmed. We often judge ourselves for the way that we feel, especially when it doesn't match what society, Google, our friends, or our family say we should feel. Many of us have a hard time adapting to changes in our moods and the outside world; the challenge is that in this life, the only thing that's constant is **change**. Of course we're anxious! No wonder we look for answers anywhere we might find them.

Throughout this book, I've shared many factors that contribute to our chronic anxiety that don't necessarily coincide with the predominant view. But I don't think I have to work too hard to convince you that the knowledge I've shared here is valuable, especially if you just take a closer look at your own experiences and relationships. However, I want to be clear that I offer this knowledge not to tell you what causes your anxiety, but rather to show you the multiple variables that contribute to the experience of anxiety. I work from the assumption that much of our chronic anxiety is a product of relationship distress, and people need to think differently to master it.

All of us are born with a certain level of chronic anxiety and differentiation of self. If we can learn to tolerate our anxiety, we can work on choosing different behaviors that help enhance who we are, rather than creating more anxiety in our lives. Becoming less anxious and more mature is an important goal that gets achieved fairly slowly. At this point in your life, you might not be as *calm* and centered as you'd like; you might get frustrated, mentally beat yourself up, and act immature more often than you'd care to admit (I know I still do). This book isn't a get-anxiety-free-quick scheme; I don't promise fast results. I want to be straight with you. Being a source of calm in an anxious world filled with complex relationships isn't an easy thing to achieve. However, learning to grow into ourselves means seeing the world from a different perspective. It means creating a better present—and, therefore, a better future—for ourselves and our loved ones. It means that no matter the circumstance, we bring the best of ourselves and remember that people define events, events don't define people.

BIBLIOGRAPHY

Amsterdam J.D., Yimei L., Soeller I., Rockwell, K., Mao, J. J., & Shults, J. (2009) "A randomized, double-blind, placebo-controlled trial of oral Matricaria recutita (chamomile) extract therapy for generalized anxiety disorder." *Journal of Clinical Psychopharmacology*, 29 (4), 378–382.

Anderson, E., & Shivakumar, G. (2013). "Effects of exercise and physical activity on anxiety." *Front Psychiatry*. Retrieved from https://www.ncbi.nlm.nih.gov/pmc/articles/PMC3632802/

Apaydin, E. A., Maher, A. R., Shanman, R., Booth, M. S., Miles, J. N. V., Sorbero, M. E., & Hempel, S. (2016). "A systematic review of St. John's wort for major depressive disorder." *Systematic Review*, 5 (148). doi: 10.1186/2Fs13643-016-0325-2

Benson S., Downey, L. A., Stough, C., Wetherall, M., Zangara, A., & Scholey, A. (2013). "An acute, double-blind, placebo-controlled cross-over study of 320 mg and 640 mg doses of Bacopa monnieri (CDRI 08) on multitasking stress reactivity and mood." *Phytotherapy Research*, 28 (4), 551-559. doi: 10.1002/ptr.5029

Boonstra E., de Kleijn, R., Colzato, L. S., Alkemade, A., Forstmann, B. U., Nieuwenhuis, S. (2015). "Neurotransmitters as food supplements: the effects of GABA on brain and behavior." *Frontiers in Psychology*, 6, doi: 10.3389/fpsyg.2015.01520

Bowen, M. (1978). *Family Therapy in Clinical Practice*. Lanham, MD: Jason Aronson.

Brown, J. (2012). *Growing Yourself Up: How to bring your best to all of life's relationships*. New South Wales, Australia: Exisle.

Cases J., Ibarra, A., Fuillere, N., Roller, M., & Sukkar, S. (2011). "Pilot trial of Melissa officinalis L. leaf extract in the treatment of volunteers suffering from mild-to-moderate anxiety disorders and sleep disturbances." *Mediterranean Journal of Nutrition and Metabolism*, 4(3), 2011-2018. doi:10.3233/s12349-010-0045-4

Chang, S. Y. (2008). "Effects of aroma hand massage on pain, state anxiety and depression in hospice patients with terminal cancer." *Taehan Kanho Hakhoe Chi*, 38(4), 493-502.

Chang, K., & Shen, C. (2011). "Aromatherapy benefits autonomic nervous system regulation for elementary school faculty in Taiwan. Evidence-Based Complementary and Alternative Medicine." Retrieved from http://www.hindawi.com/journals/ecam/2011/946537/

Chua H. C., Christensen, E. T. H., Hoestgaard-Jensen, K., Hartiadi, L. Y., Ramzan, I., Jensen, A. A., Absalom, N. L., & Chebib, M. (2016). "Kavain, the major constituent of the anxiolytic kava extract, potentiates GABA-A receptors: Functional characteristics and molecular mechanism." doi: 10.1371/journal.pone.0157700

Cropley M., Banks, A. P., Boyle, J. (2015). "The effects of Rhodiola rosea L. extract on anxiety, stress, cognition and other mood symptoms." *Phytotherapy Research*, 29(12), 1934-1939. doi:10.1002/ptr.5486

Dantas L-P., Oliveira-Ribeiro, A., de Almeida-Souza, L-M., Groppo, F-C. (2016). "Effects of Passiflora incarnata and midazolam for control of anxiety in patients undergoing dental extraction." *Oral Surgery*, 22 (1), 95-101. doi:10.4317/2Fmedoral.21140

Eunhee H., & Shin, S. (2015). "The effects of aromatherapy on sleep improvement: A systematic literature review and meta-analysis." *The Journal of Alternative and Complementary Medicine*, 21(2). doi: doi.org/10.1089/acm.2014.0113

Fiebich B. L., Knorle, R., Appel, K., Kammler, T., & Weiss, G. (2011). "Pharmacological studies in an herbal drug combination of St. John's Wort (Hypericum perforatum) and passion flower (Passiflora incarnata): In vitro and in vivo evidence of synergy between Hypericum and Passiflora in antidepressant pharmacological models." *Fitoterapia*, 82(3), 474-480. doi: 10.1016/j.fitote.2010.12.006

Gautam M., Agrawal, M., Gautam, M., Sharma, P.,Gautam, A. S., Gautam, S. (2012). "Role of antioxidants in generalized anxiety disorder and depression." *Indian Journal of Psychiatry*, 54(3), 244-247. doi: 10.4103/0019-5545.102424

Gilbert, R. (1999). *Extraordinary Relationships: A new way of thinking about human interactions*. New York, NY: John Wiley.

Jackson, P. (2006). *Sacred Hoops: spiritual lessons of a hardwood warrior*. New York, NY: Hachette Books.

John Hopkins Medicine. (2014). "Meditation for anxiety and depression." Retrieved from, https://www.hopkinsmedicine.org/news/media/releases/meditation_for_anxiety_and_depression

Jaleh M. A., Tahereh, N. G., Fatemeh, A., & Rahele, R. (2016). "Effect of combined inhalation of lavender oil, chamomile and neroli oil in vital signs of people with acute coronary syndrome." *Iranian Journal of Cardiovascular Nursing*, 5(3), 42-51. sid.ir/En/Journal/ViewPaper.aspx?ID=531831

Joseph D., & Kollareth, M. (2017). "Neuroprotective efficacy of a combination of fish oil and Bacopa monnieri against 3-nitropropionic acid induced oxidative stress in rats." *International Journal of Neurology Research,* 3(2), 349-357. doi: 10.17554/j.issn.2313-5611.2017.03.67

Keating, D.P., (2016). Born Anxious: *The Lifelong Impact of Early Life Adversity - and How to Break the Cycle.* St. Martin's Press.

Kerr, M. E., & Bowen, M. (1988). *Family Evaluation: An Approach-based on Bowen Theory.* New York, NY: Norton.

Kerr, M. E. (2020) *Bowen Theory's Secrets: Revealing the hidden life of families.* New York, NY: W.W Norton & Company.

Koulivand P. H., Ghadiri, M. K., & Gorji, A. (2013). "Lavender and the nervous system". *Evidence-Based Complementary and Alternative Medicine.* doi: dx.doi.org/10.1155/2013/681304

Karonova T. L., Andreeva, A. T., Beljaeva, O. D., Bazhenova, E. A., Globa, P. J., Vasil'eva, E. G., & Grineva, E. N. (2015). "Anxiety/depressive disorders and vitamin D status." *Zh Nevrol Psikhiatr Im S S Korsakova,* 115(10), 55-58. Retrieved from ncbi.nlm.nih.gov/pubmed/26977917

Keicolt-Glaser J. K., Belury, M. A., Andridge, R., Malarkey, W. B., & Glaser, R. (2011). "Omega-3 supplementation lowers inflammation and anxiety in medical students: A randomized controlled trial." *Brain, Behavior, and Immunity,* 25(8), 1725-1734. doi: 10.1016/j.bbi.2011.07.229

Lewis J. E, Tiozzo, E., Melillo, A. B., Leonard, S., Chen, L., Mendez, A., Woolger, J. M., & Konefal, J. (2013). "The effect of methylated vitamin B complex on depressive and anxiety symptoms and quality of life in adults with depression." doi: 10.1155/2013/621453

Maiti T., Adhikari, A., & Panda, A. (2012). "A study on evaluation of antidepressant effect of Imipramine adjunct with Ashwagandha and Bramhi." Retrieved from ijam.co.in/index. php/ijam/article/view/155/119

Möhler H. (2012). "The GABA system in anxiety and depression and its therapeutic potential." *Neuropharmacology* 62(1) 42-53. doi: 10.1016/j.neuropharm.2011.08.040

Noone, R. J., & Papero, D. V. (2015). *The Family Emotional System: An integrative concept for theory, science, and practice.* Lanham, MD: Lexington Books.

Saiyudthong, S., & Marsden, C. A. (2011). "Acute effects of bergamot oil on anxiety-related behaviour and corticosterone level in rats." *Phytotherapy Research*, 25(6), 858-62.

Shiina Y., Funabashi N., Lee K., Toyoda T., Sekine T., Honjo S. Komuro, I. (2007). "Relaxation effects of lavender aromatherapy improve coronary flow velocity reserve in healthy men evaluated by transthoracic Doppler echo-cardiography." *International Journal of Cardiology.* 129(2), 193-197.

Titelman, P. (Ed.) (2008). *Triangles: Bowen Family Systems Theory Perspectives.* New York, NY: Haworth Clinical Practice Press.

Ogawa S, et al. (2018). "Effects of L-theanine on anxiety-like behavior, cerebrospinal fluid amino acid profile, and hippocampal activity in Wistar Kyoto rats." DOI: 10.1007/s00213-017-4743-1

Pratte M. A., Ota, M., Ogura, J., Kato, K., & Kunugi, H. (2014). "An alternative treatment for anxiety: A systematic review of human trial results reported for the Ayurvedic herb Ashwagandha (Withania somnifera)." doi:10.1089/acm.2014.0177

Jorgensen, B. P., Winther, G., Kihl, P., & Nielsen, D. S. (2015). "Dietary magnesium deficiency affects gut microbiota and anxiety-like behavior in C57BL/6N mice." *Acta Neuropsychiatrica*, 27(5), 307-311.doi: 10.1017/neu.2015.10

Ritsner M. S., Miodownik, C., Ratner, Y., Shleifer, T., Mar, M., Pintov, L., & Lerner, V. (2011). "L-theanine relieves positive, activation, and anxiety symptoms in patients with schizophrenia and schizoaffective disorder: An 8-week, randomized, double-blind, placebo-controlled, 2-center study." *The Journal of Clinical Psychiatry*, 72(1). doi:10.4088/JCP.09m05324gre

Srivastava J. K., Shankar, E., & Gupta, S. (2010). "Chamomile: A herbal medicine of the past with a bright future (Review)." *Molecular Medicine Reports*, 3(6), 895-901. doi: 10.3892/mmr.2010.377

Wolynn, M. (2016). *It Didn't Start With You: How Inherited Family Trauma Shapes Who We Are And How To End The Cycle*. Penguin Publishing Group.

INDEX

ACKNOWLEDGMENTS

While many people have contributed to the development of this book, the most direct input was from Dr. Murray Bowen's brilliant theory of family systems. I am grateful to have learned about this theory in my doctoral program at Nova Southeastern University, and to have been able to study it intensely ever since.

There are several other people whose contribution to this book I'd like to acknowledge. I appreciate every one of you for how you've influenced this book, and for the lessons I never would have learned without you.

Denise Fournier, you know what I want to say and help me express it in words that will make more sense to my readers. Thank you for being with me from the beginning.

Natalie Cormier, you have been instrumental in making this book what it is. I appreciate the time and energy you put into making this book even better. Thanks for being you, and all that you do. I appreciate the encouragement and dedication you have given to me.

Edrica Richardson, you read through my entire book draft when I wasn't sure about it, and you gave me wonderful suggestions. I'm grateful for the great friend and colleague you've been to me.

Jim Rudes, thank you for reviewing Anxious for Answers, chapter by chapter, for me. I appreciate your input and help in this process. You made sure my systems thinking was accurate and useful.

Jeffrey Miller, I'm so fortunate to have the opportunity to learn from you. I'm happy that you reviewed my book and gave me so much useful feedback. Thanks to you, I have developed my systems thinking.

Olivia S. Colmer, you've always been a good friend and a wonderful colleague. Thank you for always having my back.

Corinne Dannon, you've been encouraging and a great person to go to for ideas. I am grateful for you.

Michelle Dempsey, thank you for your encouragement and positivity. The way you believe in my work means a lot to me.

To my Bowen training group, meeting with you on Saturdays was a very meaningful experience for me. I've learned so much from all of you, and am grateful to each one of you. A special thanks to Lance Simkins for reading over this book and giving me feedback. Your time is appreciated.

There's no way to overstate the contribution my clients have made to this book. I'm astonished every day by your strength and resilience. Thank you for opening up to me, and for letting me share your stories so that others can learn from your example and improve their lives.

Mom, you have always been my number one fan. I see not only my evolution in this process, but yours, too. I'm very appreciative of you and the thoughtfulness you always give about my work.

Dad, thanks for always believing in me. I will get you that plane soon.

Moises Cohen, I love you. Thank you for always being supportive of my work.

Emily and Elizabeth, my babies, I'm proud of you both and love you.

To my siblings, niece, nephews, and cousins, all of you are very special to me. I hope you find this book useful to you in some way.

To my in-laws, who are so very special to me, I'm happy we joined our families together. I am constantly learning from you.

To everyone in my life, thank you for being you and contributing what you have to this book and to my life.

185

"Dr. Ilene" S. Cohen, Ph.D. is a psychotherapist, professor, and blogger. She is also the author of the popular self-help guide, *When It's Never About You*, as well as co-author (with Rabbi Aryeh Weinstein) of *It's Within You*. She's a regular contributor to *Psychology Today*, and her work has appeared in *Psych Central* and *Tiny Buddha*, along with many other online publications. Her books and her therapy practice are fueled by a passion for helping people achieve their goals, build a strong sense of self, and lead fulfilling and meaningful lives. As president of her family's foundation, Dr. Ilene oversees myriad initiatives geared toward creating better opportunities for those in need.

To contact Dr. Ilene directly, you can visit her website, **www.doctorilene.com.**

Printed in Great Britain
by Amazon

79670805R30115